087926

THE LIBRARY
ST. MARY'S COLLEGE OF MARYLAND
ST. MARY'S CITY, MARYLAND 20686.

TWAYNE'S WORLD AUTHORS SERIES
A Survey of the World's Literature

ITALY

Carlo Golino, University of Massachusetts
EDITOR

Clemente Rebora

TWAS 521

Ink drawing by Filomena Puglisi

Clemente Rebora

CLEMENTE REBORA

By **MARGHERITA MARCHIONE**

Fairleigh Dickinson University

TWAYNE PUBLISHERS

A DIVISION OF G. K. HALL & CO., BOSTON

Copyright © 1979 by G.K. Hall & Co.

Published in 1979 by Twayne Publishers,
A Division of G. K. Hall & Co.
All Rights Reserved

Printed on permanent/durable acid-free paper and bound
in the United States of Amercia

First Printing

Library of Congress Cataloging in Publication Data

Marchione, Margherita.
Clemente Rebora.

(Twayne's world authors series ; TWAS 521 : Italy)
Bibliography: p. 173 - 76
Includes index.
1. Rebora, Clemente, 1885 - 1957–Criticism and interpretation.
PQ4839.E25Z77   851'.9'12   78-7632
ISBN 0-8057-6362-7

2-06-79

Dedicated to Giuseppe Prezzolini,
mentor and dear friend

Contents

About the Author
Preface
Chronology

1. First and Last Meeting — 15
2. Literary Panorama — 19
3. Early Life — 24
4. Idealist — 30
5. Teacher — 35
6. Friend — 41
7. *La Voce* Movement — 46
8. *Frammenti lirici* — 51
9. *Poesie varie* — 70
10. Russian Interlude — 79
11. The Ordeal of War — 88
12. *Canti anonimi* — 100
13. Mazzini's Disciple — 108
14. Mystic — 113
15. The Road to Damascus — 119
16. *Canti dell'infermità* — 125
17. *Curriculum Vitae* — 130
18. Correspondence — 138
19. Critics — 145
20. Conclusion — 150

Notes and References — 153
Selected Bibliography — 173
Index — 177

About the Author

Sister Margherita Marchione is Professor of Italian in the College of Arts and Sciences, Fairleigh Dickinson University, Madison, New Jersey. She was born in Little Ferry, New Jersey, in 1922 and received her B.A. from Georgian Court College and her M.A. and Ph.D. from Columbia University. Among the honors she has received are: Garibaldi Scholar, NDEA Grant in French, Fulbright Scholar, AMITA (American-Italian Award) Award in Education, Grand Order of Dr. Filippo Mazzei—William Paca Historical Research Medal, UNICO (Unity, Neighborliness, Integrity, Charity, Opportunity) National Rizzuto Award, Collier of the International Association of University Presidents. She has received several Fairleigh Dickinson University research grants and the New Jersey Bicentennial Commission Grant, besides the Kosciuszko Grant and the Premio della Cultura Grant. The President of Italy has conferred upon her the highest award of the Italian Republic, Cavaliere dell'Ordine della Stella della Solidarietà Italiana.

Sister Margherita has published various scholarly books (most notably *L'Imagine Tesa*, 1960, 1974, and *Twentieth Century Italian Poetry*—a bilingual anthology, 1974), and numerous essays and articles in Italian scholarly journals. Her articles have also appeared in *Italian Quarterly, The Literary Review, Forum, Italian Americana*. She has edited *Carteggio di Clemente Rebora, 1893 - 1930*, Edizioni di Storia e Letteratura, 1976, and coedited, with S. Eugene Scalia, a series of six volumes of scholarly work, *Carteggio di Giovanni Boine, 1905 - 1917* (Volume I, *Giuseppe Prezzolini*, 1971; Volume II, *Emilio Cecchi*, 1972; Volume III, 2 tomes, *Amici del Rinnovamento*, 1977; Volumes IV - V in press).

The book *Philip Mazzei: Jefferson's "Zealous Whig"* was enthusiastically received (American Institute of Italian Studies, 1975). Sister Margherita is now the editor-in-chief of *The Papers of Philip Mazzei,* a project funded by NHPRC (National Historical Publications and Records Commission). It will be a

About the Author

complete microform edition and guide, followed by several volumes of selected letters and writings in letterpress.

Besides lecturing here and abroad, Sister Margherita has made radio and television appearances. Among the many administrative posts held are: Chairman of the Foreign Language Department, Director of NDEA (National Defense Education Act) and FDU (Fairleigh Dickinson University) Italian Institutes, President of Walsh College, President of the AIIS (American Insitute of Italian Studies), member of the Executive Council of the AIHA (American Italian Historical Association), a member of the NJCHRC (New Jersey Catholic Historical Records Commission) and also of the NJHC (New Jersey Historical Commission). A member of many other organizations—local, national, and international—she is included in Who's Who of American Women, Who's Who among Authors and Journalists, the Directory of American Scholars, the National Register of Prominent Americans and International Notables, Outstanding Educators of America, The World Who's Who of Women.

Preface

This book is offered to the general reader in an attempt to portray, as briefly as possible, Clemente Rebora, the literary figure, against the background of his spiritual itinerary. I have endeavored to recreate the historical context through an essential biography and an analysis of his poetic production, with attention to the many interrelations that bind his lyrics to his prose and letters.

In order to explain Rebora's spiritual development, I have attempted to probe into his innermost thoughts, his intimate considerations, the turmoil and conflicts of his soul and have proceeded through such an analysis to an interpretation of his poetry through his correspondence. To avoid a superficial and unrealistic explanation of his life it has been necessary to make use of a large portion of these letters, which have value not only for the originality of their language and style—seldom relaxed, at times restless and tormented, and not infrequently almost poetic, as he outlines his deepest feelings—but also for their autobiographical and spiritual elements. They reveal his life as a teacher, lecturer, and writer, as well as his friends, his interest in Tagore, his conversion to the Catholic faith.

Poetry is seldom, if ever, a spontaneous product. The purely lyrical values of a poet are born and nurtured and definitely grow in a vaster, more intimate field of resonance, that is, a human one. The poetic world proceeds from a human world, just as a flower comes from the earth with the gardener's tender care. In Rebora, too, its roots are deep and varied.

Because of limited space, much valuable information has been omitted in writing about Rebora, the man and the poet. The sources used were, of course, the entire literary production of Rebora (poems, prose, translations) and the numerous writings on his poetry. To these are to be added such special sources as his letters (some never before published) written to relatives and friends; my conversations with Rebora during my three-month stay in Stresa in the summer of 1957; my conversations and correspondence with his friends and relatives and with the leading critics of the Italian literary world.[1]

I wish to thank the following publishers for kind permission to quote from my books, namely *L'Imagine Tesa* and *Twentieth Century Italian Poetry,* the first published by Edizioni di Storia e Letteratura (Rome, 1960, 1974) and the other by Fairleigh Dickinson Press (Rutherford, N.J., 1974). All translations are my own.

I am grateful to Rebora's family and friends and to the critics, whose unselfish generosity have enabled me to write about him. I owe very special thanks to Dr. S. Eugene Scalia for his encouragement and help during the preparation of this book and to Claire Murray for her kind assistance in reading the manuscript. I am also grateful to Dr. Carlo Golino for his supervision of the work and to Sister Filomena Puglisi for the ink sketch of Clemente Rebora. Above all, I am indebted to Giuseppe Prezzolini, who introduced me to the poet more than twenty years ago.

MARGHERITA MARCHIONE

Fairleigh Dickinson University

Chronology

1885 Born in Milan, Via Aldo Manuzio 15, on January 6; baptized in the Church of Santa Francesca Romano.
1892 Attends elementary school at Via Alessandro Tadino.
1897 Attends ginnasio-liceo "Parini."
1900 Writes the poem "Anima errante."
1903 Begins medical studies at the University of Pavia.
1904 Continues studies at the Accademia Scientifico-Letteraria (University of Milan).
1905 Interrupts studies for military training.
1909 Presents dissertation on Romagnosi under the historian Gioacchino Volpe.
1910 Receives doctorate in Letters. Teaches in Milan, Treviglio, Novara. Publishes thesis, "Per un Leopardi mal noto," in *Rivista d'Italia*.
1911 Publishes dissertation, "G. D. Romagnosi nel pensiero del Risorgimento," in *Rivista d'Italia*.
1913 Publishes book *Frammenti lirici*, Libreria della Voce.
1914 Continues publishing articles and poems in *La Voce, La Grande Illustrazione, Riviera Ligure*.
1915 Becomes an officer in World War I. Publishes poem in *Almanacco della Voce*.
1916 Publishes poetic prose writings in *La Lettura, La Brigata, Riviera Ligure*.
1917 Continues publications in *La Tempra, La Diana*.
1918 Publishes poems in *La Raccolta*.
1919 Translates Andreyev's *Lazarus and Other Short Stories*. Publishes book review in *L'Illustrazione Italiana*. Discontinues teaching in government school system.
1920 Translates Tolstoi's *Family Happiness*.
1922 Publishes second volume of poetry, *Canti anonimi*. Translates Gogol's *The Overcoat*. Translates the English tale *Janârdana*.
1923 Publishes *Janârdana* with Commentary.

1924 Teaches in various cultural centers and private schools during the next six years.
1927 Publishes "Versi" in *Il Convegno*.
1929 Enters the Catholic Church on November 24.
1930 Publishes article in *Bollettino del Gruppo d'Azione*.
1931 Joins the Rosmini Fathers as a novice at Domodossola.
1933 Studies theology and makes religious profession.
1936 Ordained a priest and becomes prefect of the scholastics.
1938 Made spiritual director at the Collegio Mellerio-Rosmini in Domodossola.
1943 Transferred to the Rosmini Institute in Torino and becomes its spiritual director.
1946 Named assistant pastor in Rovereto.
1947 Publishes *Le Poesie*.
1949 Publishes poetry in *La Fiera Letteraria*.
1951 Contributes articles to *Charitas*.
1955 Publishes *Via Crucis* and *Curriculum Vitae*.
1956 Receives "Cittadella" award.
1957 Publishes *Canti dell'Infermità*. Dies in Stresa on November 1.

CHAPTER 1

First and Last Meeting

Clemente Rebora—whom I still see as a most handsome and dear youth, of velvety eyes, frank expression, enchanting words; with his family he seemed to be one of the best products of the country which was then mine. (Letter from Professor Giuseppe Prezzolini, July 7, 1957 to Margherita Marchione)

WHEN I FIRST MET CLEMENTE REBORA THE MAN—THE POET I already knew—he lay almost lifeless on his bed in the Stresa convent of the Rosmini Fathers, of which he was a member. One would have thought him a corpse had it not been for the beautiful smile and the luminous, penetrating eyes which greeted me and encouraged me to speak. I did not see Professor Giuseppe Prezzolini's "most handsome and dear youth, of velvety eyes, frank expression, enchanting words." What I saw was a bedridden man wasted by arteriosclerosis, speaking only with difficulty. He remembered the letters I had written him and had been expecting me. I immediately conveyed greetings from Prezzolini, adding that he still admired his poetry and had suggested that I write about it. I then showed him photostatic copies of letters he had written to Prezzolini from 1909 to 1914, and told him of the wonderful response at Columbia University to my lecture on his poetry.

During my sojourn in Stresa, I was privileged to visit Clemente Rebora frequently. Rain or shine I climbed the steep hill that led to the Collegio Rosmini every day. And regularly I reported about my trips through Italy, the interviews, the letters written, the letters received—all my experiences while searching for information about his past, how everyone was anxious to contribute. Friends: Angelo Monteverdi of the University of Rome and Antonio Banfi, a Communist senator; journalists, artists, professors, literary critics: Falqui of Rome's *Il Tempo*, Fabiani of *Il Popolo* of Milan, and Carrà, Saggio, Galletti, Gallarati Scotti, his brother Piero Rebora—all of Milan; Cascella of Portofino, Gioacchino Volpe of Rome; Cesare Angelini of Pavia. How he listened, enraptured, when I told of my visit to the Vatican and asked the Holy Father[1] for a special blessing that my work on Clemente Rebora might be successful!

As I gazed at the priest Rebora during my last visit (August 16, 1957) I recalled my letter to him for his feast day. I had also sent him a spiritual bouquet and a small bookmark on which was painted a chalice. He had answered: "From my sick bed, with emotion and with grateful surprise, I received your dear wishes, and besides, the prayerful spiritual bouquet, and also the loving drawing of my priestly emblem. Thank you, and continue to keep me in the treasure chest of your prayers. I cannot but send you my blessing, which may always remain in your soul, and upon all you do in thought and work for the glory of God and of His Christ Jesus. I will send you a poem, the last, *"Il Natale* [Christmas]."[2]

Before leaving his bedside I spoke about Professor Prezzolini's recent visit to him on July 20th. The two friends had been separated for forty-five years! "But you, Father, did you remember Prezzolini all these years?" I inquired. "Oh, yes, my dear, we have been closely associated. . . . I love Prezzolini." Then Rebora blessed me for the last time.

During the next few weeks the poet's sufferings became more intense. Soon news arrived from Pavia: "Our Rebora, 'your poet,' passed away this morning. I think Don Clemente, among his last thoughts and visions of this earthly life which he was about to leave, has had those of a dear little Sister who had come from America to concern herself about him, to gather together all that the best Italians thought of him, and to celebrate his memory. The merit is also our dear Prezzolini's, who, as he evaluated his appearance on the literary scene, so too has assisted him in his departure, entrusting you to speak about him. A work of poetry and, at the same time, of compassion which weaves itself into the mysterious ways of the spirit and is transformed into good for the one who has promoted it and for the one who has fulfilled it."[3]

First and Last Meeting

About the same time Rebora's last message to me, dated October 29, arrived. His nurse had written: "I cannot tell you how moved Father was on receiving your letter." And months later he explained that he was surprised to notice that Don Clemente "became unusually animated whenever he heard your name and there was no need to help him remember, as so often happened."[4]

Rebora is no longer with us. He did not leave a complete autobiography. His *Curriculum Vitae* may be called a poetic autobiography, but it practically ignores the years prior to his conversion at the age of forty-four. How, then, is one to explain his spiritual development, the joys and anguish of his soul? How can one comprehend his philosophy of life during this period?

One can probe into his innermost thoughts, his intimate considerations, the turmoil and conflicts of his soul and proceed through such an analysis to an intepretation of his poetry through his correspondence.[5]

Copies of Rebora's correspondence were not acquired without a struggle. It required a great deal of courage to appear boldly before critics, professors, the nobility, with or without appointments. I found myself in not a few precarious situations. Once I was refused admittance to the palace of a duke (the servants thought I was seeking alms). When the duke heard about this incident, he generously made amends. He not only invited me to dinner but insisted that I meet one of Rebora's former friends—a classmate of his, an invaluable interpreter of the first young Rebora, later a dear friend of mine, who, I hope and pray, finally understood the new Rebora, the Rebora reborn in Christ.

Unforgettable were the hours spent in Pavia, at the Collegio Borromeo, in the company of Cesare Angelini, whom Papini[6] called "twice consecrated: to the Word that became flesh and to the word that attempts to become beauty."

I wrote to all those I could not visit. They answered with much kindness—Anceschi, Betocchi, Casnati, Cecchi, Costanzo, Montale, Spagnoletti, Titta Rosa. It was easy to perceive their love and respect and admiration for Clemente Rebora.

And of another thing I became immediately aware. I, an outsider, for the first time a timid visitor in the "republic of letters," was pleasantly surprised to notice always and everywhere a sense of fraternity and unselfish generosity with which the leading citizens of the country welcomed me, treated me as one of them, aided me in all possible ways.

To understand Rebora and his work one could not possibly be satisfied with a superficial, unrealistic, stultified explanation of his life. The study of his poems and correspondence, the revealing memories of relatives, friends, students, and former associates, give one the courage to write about Rebora—the man and the poet—with a fair chance of success. Whether I have succeeded, I do not know. But, accepting the difficult and fascinating challenge, I have tried to, lovingly and honestly.

CHAPTER 2

Literary Panorama

THE "DISCOVERY" OF THE REALITY OF ITALIAN LIFE, THE NEW social standards, the deepening of a national consciousness—all led toward the rebirth of Italian poetry at the turn of the century.

During Rebora's youth the Italian literary scene was dominated by three poets—Giosuè Carducci,[1] Giovanni Pascoli,[2] Gabriele D'Annunzio.[3] They were undeniably great, but their imitators risked suffocating Italian poetry with metrical rehashings. There were *carducciani, pascoliani, dannunziani,* but there was no longer anyone of the actual stature of Carducci, Pascoli, or D'Annunzio. There were rhetoricians, whose verses emphasized style often at the expense of thought. There were academicians, who adhered to conventional themes. Romanticism and Classicism were being revived with their old themes, motifs, forms and accents. Much in the literature of the first decade, then, was empty rhetoric, form without content.

The *pascoliani* had employed many of Pascoli's techniques without success. The *dannunziani* had emptied their words of all humanity to inflate them with mere breath. The *carducciani* had turned theirs into stylized vociferation and clamor. A reaction was inevitable. It began by ridiculing these hackneyed, complicated, and inflated forms. In the hope of restoring simplicity and conversational tone, members of the reaction satirized the high-flown, archaic language of the imitators. The reaction was called Crepuscolarism.[4] Its chief representatives were Sergio Corazzini,[5] Marino Moretti,[6] Guido Gozzano,[7] and Aldo Palazzeschi.[8] They depicted the ordinary and the trivial in a melancholy mood, using simple words and humble themes. Their intention was good, but with them came the danger of a new rhetoric. Putting too much trust in the naked, unadorned word (and theme), they ended up degrading and corrupting it with their trifling (coquetry). As a poetic current, Crepuscolarism (also called Provincialism) fast became a clever, witty, often foolish game.

I *Futurism*

Another reaction took the name of Futurism. It rejected the entire past, revolutionizing grammar and proclaiming the autonomy of words *(parole in libertà)*. Futurism's best-known exponent, Filippo Tommaso Marinetti,[9] and his followers were not without poetic sensibility. In their eagerness to ignore grammar, literary forms, and tradition, they lacked a sense of moderation and earnestness. Like Crepuscolarism, Futurism lost itself in a wild and unhealthy rhetoric. Its champions—Marinetti, Corrado Govoni,[10] Paolo Buzzi[11] —were so involved in their war on conventionalism that they did not realize this was happening. It is to be noted that the Futurists did not only war against Carduccianism, Pascolianism, and Dannunzianism but the cults of many others in the literary world. Yet, in the interest of truth, it must be said that one good poem of Carducci, Pascoli, D'Annunzio, or Guido Gozzano has more poetic value than all the multicolored but often insolent and incoherent productions of the Futurists.

Both Crepuscolarism and Futurism succeeded, however, in focusing attention on problems of vital importance for the new generation. These two movements served to wrest Italian poetry from the hands of rhetoricians and academicians and direct it toward originality and sincerity. Futurism had another aim—to make Italian poetry a European experience. Carducci, Pascoli, and D'Annunzio had left Italian poetry within the province: Carducci with the myth of the nation, Pascoli with the myth of Arcadia, D'Annunzio—inspired by Nietzsche and the Parnassians —with that of sensuality and heroism.

Perhaps one can say that literary Italy was a province of literary France; what may be regarded as antitraditionalism is often but an imitation or echo of the latest Parisian literary fad or genius. D'Annunzio, for example, imitated the Parisians, both as poet and novelist. Meanwhile, in this period of confusion there was much research and ferment, which has been called "semiserious experimentalism in the name of novelty that had repercussions throughout the whole of Europe."[12]

Futurism influenced the political sphere and became an organ for intervention in World War I. Subsequently there followed a period of moral awakening in Italy. According to Giacinto Spagnoletti:[13]

In a certain sense the Futurists would have been able to avoid deceiving themselves if they had paid attention—not to the new means given to man by scientific progress—but to the human *coscienza* [consciousness and conscience] which had to dominate these means. They deceived themselves above all by making their own the most absurd illusions promulgated by the decadence, imagining some energy or dignity would be released by war and destruction. So too they fancied that by destroying the language some force or glory would be restored to it.

It was high time to embrace vaster myths, somewhat after the manner of, say, the nineteenth-century French poet Baudelaire. Futurism was the product of the times, born of the growing tendency to break the chains of nineteenth-century formalism. Unfortunately the aim of the Futurists was greater than their ability; their wings could not sustain the flight.

Both movements rejected the literary values and standards of their times, which were based on weak, passive, inert imitation, and affirmed the urgency of renovation. A militant Italian culture was taking its stand against the rhetoric of nineteenth-century poetry—still Carduccian, Pascolian, and Dannunzian. Its representatives, whether Crepuscolarists or Futurists, were accomplishing the useful function of opening new roads, of searching for a new idiom—originality. They were seeking a new sincerity through a European experience.

II La Voce

And there was a third reaction. Piero Jahier, Giovanni Boine, Clemente Rebora, Arturo Onofri, Dino Campana, and Carlo Michaelstädter were among others also clamoring for reform. Many of them belonged to the group of *La Voce*,[14] the literary review founded in 1908 that called for action and awareness of social conditions; but, *vociani* or not, they were all going in one direction: all were searching for a new manner of expression; all were intensely preoccupied with spiritual values and moral issues.

Italian culture integrated into the life of the nation. The

movement assumed a true significance not only in relation to the arts and literature, but on a moral plane as well. *La Voce* enlisted the support of the leading figures in Italy—men who differed not only in character but in political and philosophical thought.

There were also notable differences among the *vociani,* particularly if one includes Giovanni Papini[15] and Ardengo Soffici.[16] For them and for Campana,[17] the aesthetic revolution had a predominantly lyrical significance. For Rebora, Onofri,[18] Boine,[19] and Jahier[20] it had a moral, or at least a predominantly moral, one. These last shared a common metaphysical concern, but Rebora's personality was more clearly religious; Onofri's more complicated by mystical leanings; and Jahier's and Boine's more philosophical and moralistic.

Returning to what these poets had in common, one notes that the moralists retained to some extent a lyrical inspiration, for their religious faith was also poetry; and the lyricists were not devoid of a moralistic concern, for the new revolution was also seeking new ideas and new answers in its search for sincerity. They were all lyricists in the final analysis: the distinguishing mark of their breed is precisely a metaphysical lyricism. All discovered new and deeper meanings that stirred the poet in them. In all of them, the word became heavy, mysterious, and dark with a darkness that gave light to the *initiated.* The importance is transferred from *things* and *motives* to the word, which seems an instrument discovered for the first time. The word was for them not so much form as substance. It acquired almost religious significance: it operated, created, consecrated; it became image and life.

III *Hermetic Poets*

The poetic revolution was most successfully carried out by the so-called "Hermetic" poets.[21] They were able to bring Italian poetry into the great European experience without making it less Italian in the process. Theirs is the credit for having promoted the true and full renovation which was to begin with Giuseppe Ungaretti[22] and his *Allegria dei naufragi* (1919) and continue with Vincenzo Cardarelli,[23] Eugenio Montale,[24] and Salvatore Quasimodo.[25] Their works are proof that Italian poetry has finally moved toward universal values in examples of high artistic purity. While essentially new and modern, this poetry returned to the best Italian traditions—to Giacomo Leopardi[26] and from Leopardi to Francesco Petrarca[27] and even to the *Dolce Stil Novo;*[28] and in Clemente Rebora's case, whose roots were not literary but mystical and philosophical, to Jacopone da Todi.[29]

The spiritual vacuum of this period is particularly evident in Clemente Rebora, who, according to Carlo Golino, "best personifies the religious crisis of his generation, which, although it displayed a religious sense, had entertained few religious beliefs. Rebora's poetry seems to imply that the spiritual aridity of the present is made bearable by an unshakable belief that the future will bring a new Word to fill the vacuum."[30]

Rebora, who harmoniously combined the qualitities of poet and prose writer, is considered a "key figure" in the Italian literary revolution of the twentieth century. He contributed actively to the reactivation of Italian poetry about 1910 - 1915, a renewal that must be understood as preceding, even though immediately, the rebirth of the new poetry.[31]

CHAPTER 3

Early Life

CLEMENTE REBORA WAS A MAN WHOSE GREATEST CONCERN IN LIFE was not the fitting together of words to produce pleasant sounds or harmonious rhythm, but the finding of truth and the realization of goodness. He was representative of a generation of Italian intellectuals who, although born in a country so traditionally Catholic, had been drawn away from the Catholic Church by the religious liberalism and political anticlericalism of the Risorgimento and the vague mysticism and idealism of Giuseppe Mazzini.[1] However, after much wandering, he did return to the Church as a Rosmini[2] Father. His writings are a manifestation of his spiritual struggles while searching for the real meaning of life, a higher reason for living and acting in a world that seemed hopelessly chaotic.

As with every poet, a knowledge of the biographical elements of his life—his mental and spiritual makeup—is indispensable for a proper understanding of his poetry. And all the more so in his case, since poetry and prose were for him the means to face his own problems, to express his conflicts, to cry out his own desolation, or to communicate his happiness and joy to others.

Clemente Rebora was born in Milan, Italy, on January 6, 1885, the fifth of seven children. His parents were freethinking, well educated, well regarded members of the middle class. His father was a business executive. A follower of Mazzini and ardent patriot, he had fought with Giuseppe Garibaldi[3] at Mentana in 1867.

Rebora's mother, a writer of verse, brought up her children in an atmosphere of poetry, music, and art. But they had no religion, no faith in the traditional sense of the word. As a boy Rebora was a lover of solitude and enjoyed the company of simple folk, in the open air, amid the serene surroundings of

Early Life

nature. He deeply loved his country friends, especially Carlo Galbusera, an old farmer from Calolzio, a small town near Lecco where the Rebora family spent their summers. Instead of spending time with his younger friends, young Rebora followed the farmer as he worked in the fields and in the gardens. He would unburden himself with Carlo, so much so that whenever his mother reprimanded him, he would retort: "No, mother, that's not what Carlo said!"

One finds in Rebora's poem *"Clemente, non fare così!"* a description of his boyhood pranks, his fantasies, his constant mischief with the domestic help, which consisted of breaking dishes, and building towers of glasses, then causing them to tumble down.

Through the poem, Rebora tells us that, with the arrival of his father, things changed; he was sent off to bed, with only his mother's kiss. Soon after his mischief, he wrote a letter to his parents, expressing sadness at offending them and promising to be a "serious, good and exemplary young man."[4]

I Early Studies

Even in his early years, Rebora was deeply sensitive. He regretted having to return to his studies after spending "a delicious period of leisure at Menaggio, enraptured by the calmness of the lake [Lake Como] and the joy of wonderful companions."[5]

In 1903 Rebora began studying medicine at the University of Pavia. But after the first lessons in anatomy, he realized that medicine was not his calling. So he enrolled at the Accademia Scientifico-Letteraria in Milan. There he joined a group of students who called themselves "La Paglia."[6] They gathered together to study and to discuss their ideals and philosophies. It was a period of study and fun, of joy and serenity, of music and contemplation.

Several members of "La Paglia" later distinguished themselves in the academic world: Antonio Banfi, Angelo Monteverdi, Lavinia Mazzucchetti.[7] The group disbanded in 1906 when one of them married, and Rebora sadly lamented the dissolution of "such a nucleus of characters so full of interests and of originality as 'La Paglia.' " He considered it a shame that it should fold up without future hope of revival.[8]

But they continued to meet in small groups. Rebora's correspondence reveals that he constantly depended on his friends' advice. He was transformed by them, became meek under the spell of their friendship, and was comforted by their exquisite goodness and tender affection. He compared himself to "Diogenes without a lantern."[9]

After attending a performance of Wagner's *Tristan and Isolde,* some of his friends began to notice Rebora's spirit of rebellion. Full of anguish yet anxious to live, he noted in a letter to Daria Malaguzzi that "life is worth living, if only to be annihilated by titans, by divinities frightfully proud in their beauty. God, how is it possible that poor flesh can vibrate with such marvelous bewilderment, can whirl a world of wonders in its blood and in its nerves, in an oblivion so perfect and sublime and absolute that it can identify itself with the recollection itself, with the knowledge itself?"[10]

In this letter Rebora confronts Daria with the question: "Where is the 'calm serenity of the entire being' which you speak about? The Greek harmony of equilibrium? I'm not acquainted with it. Either I leap or I lie down. I don't know anything else. Perpetually I tend toward something that will never be; now and then I exult with creatures who excite me and whom I shall never be able to notice in the reality of mankind. That is the main source of my perpetual anguish, the beguiling and vain torment! Everything slips away from me; even my will, which at times also dominates me savagely."[11]

As Rebora was examining his life-style, he continued his studies at the Accademia. He began to analyze his actions. Through self-study he questioned himself. Did he possess the necessary qualities and intuition to continue his study of music? Was he condemning himself foolishly? Were the daily insignificant happenings of university life, the trifles that obscured the important things of the spirit worthy of his interest? Rebora's rebellious outbursts, so common in the past, gradually diminished. But he still depended on his friends' sympathetic understanding and wrote: *"Adaptation to the environment:* that is the most wicked law ruling man. Yet the most profound, most spiritually indissoluble, most tacit and conscious friendship binds our souls in an infinite sense of attraction."[12] Rebora would expose his sentiments whenever he felt depressed and dissatisfied with himself, his work, or life in

Early Life

general. He told Daria of his sorrow that she was no longer in Milan to keep "La Paglia" united, and that he sadly felt the loss of Banfi's and Monteverdi's affection. He blamed himself, because "such good and beautiful souls could not of themselves forsake me."[13]

When Daria left Milan, Rebora found affinity with Mariuccia Zuccante, with whom he was united by the same noble aspirations. She shared his sorrows and his joys very intimately. In describing these spiritual encounters he used expressions that are similar to those in his lyric fragments. He spoke of freeing his soul, which he called "savage indomitable lioness [*selvaggia leonessa indomabile*], toward other beautiful souls in the infinite [*verso le altre anime belle nell'infinito*]." Rebora blessed the terrible anguish, the evils, and the sorrows which he claimed made him a divinity: "Only we in this infinite, only a few of us, can purify ourselves contemplating indescribable marvels; the wicked and the inept can no longer touch us." He claimed that when his soul was in ecstasy he no longer feared anything or anybody; nor could the wicked, the cowardly, the mediocre harm him.[14]

II Love for Music

In another letter to Daria of September 18 Rebora writes in the same vein, as he tries to ignore his desperate feelings and proposes to act and free himself from the nausea of long days by means of sounds, since he had "the gift to elevate himself above all with the universal mysterious truth of music, that intones the voices either tragic or vigorous or interminable of his soul which deigns to reproduce an infinity and to feel itself thus uselessly beautiful. Poetry also, if it wants to conquer me, must flow profoundly musical; even philosophy is oriented in me in a harmony of necessity; and while I drown, I still send forth a yell: all is music . . . even the deep buzzing of the tedium that I define: the combination of aspirations and of needs (chiefly affective), not satisfied."[15]

Rebora loved music, a love which, more than anything else, eventually drove him to live with a Russian concert pianist named Lydia Natus. His love for music began as a child when he would improvise at the piano, and it increased as he grew older. Often because of his need for expression he preferred to remain in Milan in the summer heat, in solitude, as he wrote to his friend Monteverdi,[16] "to experience the great fire that rages within me, for the time being a destroyer without light." But it was a semicloistered life from which he would escape whenever impelled by the irresistible desire for country life.

In 1907, Rebora accepted his harmony instructor's cordial invitation to spend eight delightful days in the Seriana Valley, enjoying the beauty of nature. He expressed his sentiments to his friends: "And I, pitchforking my will, (What a determinist!) shall ride against boredom toward the unattainable; (for such Don Quixote transformations, one needs a new Cervantes. Friends, study me and you will derive much amusement!)."

The words "against boredom" *(contro la noia)* immediately call to mind Rebora's poem about the sidetracked empty car which "unleashes the eternal against boredom, / opens toward love a vast expanse."[17]

In 1952 during an interview[18] Rebora stated: "I was much attracted to music, but music did me more harm than good." No doubt he now regretted, in the light of his priestly conscience, his cohabitation with the Russian pianist as painfully sinful. And in his *Curriculum Vitae* he wrote: "I proudly would imagine myself/ famous as a musician, poet and sage,/ but what discouragement came thereafter!"

III *Self-Portrait*

When the time came for Rebora to serve the required two-year period of military service in Brescia, a city not far from Milan, he continued his studies, though he had no faith in himself and in his academic future.[19] Upset by anxiety and the annoyance of departure, he meditated on the hardships that awaited him "with a strange bitter hope, almost with a desire for tragedy. . . ."[20] His letters—which give us a self-portrait, at times ironic, at times sad, at times happy—reveal a period of exaltation and depression, of enthusiasm and discouragement. Army life made him "something that suffers without ideas," a "strange type of a person" who "must be bridled"[21] and requires a quiet environment, not the shouting and arguing in all the dialects of Italy that he experienced in the barracks!

Rebora's self-portrait continued. He wrote to friends telling them that he wanted to be known as "a jovial and happy

Rebora," with the hope that they would forget the pessimist[22] who had buried himself "like a broken object in the mud of no further use."[23] After dutifully passing two of his exams, his letters announced that he had been "weighed and checked and thoroughly tested by the school that unfortunately is life." He disagreed with the entire educational testing system, "with a society that expected a student to pass every time he breathes, with those having no right to declare with cruelty, pettiness and hypocritical solemnity: You are worthy, you are not, you are not worth much. . . ."[24]

Rebora evaluated himself as empty, dull, colorless, amorphous, similar in every way to a castoff suit. He could not explain the reason for such sentiments and simply told Monteverdi[25] that he knew nothing and was sure that he would never do anything worthy of his friends. He warned him therefore not to be surprised at what he would do in the future. After all, time would make him a "good man," and he would be able then to laugh at the explosions of his "divine anger."

Mountain climbing was his favorite pastime during that period. Instead of studying and preparing a long-overdue bibliography, he dreamed about the three days he spent in the Alps, from the glaciers of Monte Rosa to the Simplon Pass, with unconquerable vigor, forgetful of every other thing and inebriated only with music, as though he were "a hero in a triumphal march."[26]

With his friends, Rebora enjoyed a magnificent experience on the Bernina and Roseg glaciers on another occasion and found it absolutely impossible to bend his head over books and study for exams after having plowed through the great luminous valley, after having breathed the mountain air, after having had such beautiful adventurous freedom![27] Only an alpinist could understand his feelings when, despite violent weather and falling snow in the Valle d'Aosta, he scaled the glaciers and rocky mountains of the Alps.

CHAPTER 4

Idealist

THE TAPESTRY OF REBORA'S PHILOSOPHY MAY BE TRACED IN HIS poetry, as in "Wasted Days" *(Giorni dispersi):*

> O mighty for human progress
> ineluctable certainty of truth,
> weave, weave your threads into the cloth
> which in its texture is solidly history
> and in its pattern is eternally God:
> but thus, blind and slothful,
> between death and death vile fleeting rhythm
> I too will have made you; I too.

In September 1909, Rebora went to Loveno on Lake Como with his books and notes on Giandomenico Romagnosi[1] in order to concentrate on his thesis. The task frightened him. He was suffering from fatigue. Not only was he unable to work but he became desperate. He could no longer endure the "Illuministic" world in which he was raised and educated. He could not resolve his inner conflicts—between human life and nature, imagination and reason, man and God. In an effort to end his life, he climbed a mountain (1,800 meters) where he exposed himself to the cold and deliberately ate poisonous mushrooms. He became very ill and then, in fifteen days, he wrote his dissertation on Romagnosi.

I *Father and Son*

For years there had been a barrier between Rebora and his father, whom he profoundly admired and venerated. He compared their relationship to "two adjoining houses with closed windows." When his father visited him in Loveno and accused

Idealist

him of having made himself "the laughingstock of men," Rebora wrote a letter on October 22, 1909, stating that he had been wounded in what was most intimate and sacred in him. He pleaded with his father to accept his remarks with the same sincere frankness with which his soul dictated them. While he recognized that human perfection is rigid and demanding, he felt that his father's accusations were unjust. He would not agree that he lacked a *sound* and *strong* will. True, he felt bewildered, and sought help for a moment, being alone, and overworked. But he was accomplishing this task out of a sense of *duty*. He compared his condition with *nature,* of which reason is but a very humble interpreter. It has its storms and its convulsions. So too, after a year of assiduous, profound study of the very thinkers most dear to his father, he had also discovered their innermost core. For example, in Romagnosi, the true and most powerful initiator of the positivistic movement in Italy, Rebora discovered a tempestuous youth of *ideas* and *sentiments.* He learned that Romagnosi too lost his nice *self-control*. He contended that the loss of *self-control* happens to all those who have a profound consciousness of life and tend toward the search for Truth, remaking the universe in themselves.

In this letter to his father, which clearly reveals the young Rebora's character, he continued:

I am with Buddha, Christ, Dante, Bruno (look at his *Heroici furori*) [*The Heroic Frenzies*],[2] Vico,[3] Alfieri,[4] and Leopardi; modestly according to my stature. I'm not making a profession of faith, which would be useless; I respect your way of thinking which has been able to sustain you so marvelously and as your son I cannot do otherwise.

Only, as a man, I vindicate my integrity of conscience and will, an integrity guarded and strengthened tenaciously and fearlessly with thrashing and reprimands to maintain it as I wished, I vindicate my self-control since, from the time I began to reason, I have imposed on myself a severe and perennial anatomy of my whole being to render my soul terse and ample, in the midst of so much carousing that I saw among my companions; and I vindicate nothing else, but I shall say that I was very much hurt by your words: *to make oneself the laughingstock of men and of things or sentiments;* and that encouraging me to perform my duty and above all to have *affection* toward mother!

Forgive me if I may have used a disrespectful polemical tone. Look inside me and you may see all of me and perhaps also as you would like me to be.

Perhaps it is the destiny of whoever tends toward the good and toward ideals beyond the ordinary to appear either crazy or odd or something worse.[5]

When his strength returned, Rebora begged his father's permission to remain there in Loveno, calling it a paradise from which he would never like to part. He hoped that through this experience they would be united spiritually and that there would be no bitterness between them. He wished that his goodness would surround his father more intensely than ever, and he begged to be forgiven.

II *Dissertation on Romagnosi*

It was at the suggestion of his mentor Gioacchino Volpe that Rebora wrote his dissertation on *G. D. Romagnosi nel pensiero del Risorgimento,* part of which was later published in *Rivista d'Italia* in 1911.[6]

When this work was quoted by G. A. Belloni in *Saggi sul Romagnosi* in 1940, Rebora deemed it necessary to write a statement of retraction for this article which reflected his early education. While he had written it in good faith—a task which made him so desperate that he contemplated suicide—he had unconsciously idealized Romagnosi and his philosophy, attributing to him "a most penetrating historical sense" rather than original thought. Commenting on his philosophical thought, Rebora speaks of "a secret force, invisible and spontaneous, which exists in the soul and heart of each human individual." Similar ideas appear in Rebora's lyric fragments; for example, in "Through the acrid flow of the minutes," *(Per l'acre fluir dei minuti):* "Comes the idea with dead breath,/ the idea that on coming back/ drags along a fact; and forever." The same may be said of the poem "Suffering" *(Soffrire):* "Contrastingly, the idea holding within the all/ appears tragic where it ranges,/ as does nature that creates without me."

Rebora envisioned his dissertation on Romagnosi as a series of articles to be published in *La Voce.* His manuscript consisted of approximately five hundred pages in which he shows the philosopher's importance in the "history and function of the Idealist movement of our national civic and political rebirth." In the preface and the introduction he tries "to show the political currents of the XVIII Century, necessary to the understanding of the Romagnosian apparition and phenomenon." The first chapter concerns an *interior* biography of Romagnosi, focusing on his function as educator and molder of healthy, serious, active characters, and vindicating also "the element of vitality and practical tradition hidden under the rigid and pompous mantle of his abstractly utopistic theorizing."[7]

Rebora was deeply affected by his study of Romagnosi, as is shown by his correspondence. On November 2, 1912, he expressed to Monteverdi his belief that only if we are worthy of the exigencies that strengthen and animate us to live within our center of gravitation will all around us acquire a significance that widens space, time, things in a creative and divine revelation. And to Lavinia Mazzucchetti, anxious to hear about her life in Germany, as an Italian and as a human being, he speaks of the eternal reality of life, so terribly interesting in all of its aspects, adding: "But to feel its divinity would require what many strange young men of today feel they lack. It is difficult to get to be anything like Mazzini, and even he managed it with difficulty."[8]

III *The Idealist*

Louis Chadourne was the first critic to call Rebora an idealist,[9] in his review of *Frammenti lirici* in *France-Italie:* "We find here, rather than a *vision,* a *conception* of the world. The spectacle of the universe suggests to the author more thoughts than images. This poet is an idealist-philosopher (in the precise meaning of the word)."[10] Later Emilio Cecchi reviewed Rebora's poetry in *La Tribuna:* "Rebora is weakly an idealistic poet, inasmuch as he is mechanically sure of the functioning of the *Idea,* and not at all a constrained, shocked, almost ravished assertor of the *Idea;* inasmuch as in other words, the *Idea* in him is never energetically denied, compromised."[11]

Thirty years after it appeared in *Rivista d'Italia,* Rebora disowned his work on Romagnosi. In a letter to his brother Piero (July 1, 1946), he says that at the time of his conversion, not only had he destroyed his dissertation together with all his early writings, but in 1941 he had disowned his statements on Romagnosi when his study was being used by others to attack Antonio Rosmini. As a newborn Catholic, Rebora had enough grounds to find fault with Romagnosi, an anti-Catholic.

Only seventy-six pages of Rebora's research on Romagnosi had been printed. However, in his letter to Prezzolini, Rebora explained that the two incomplete chapters were on the reconstruction of Romagnosi's encyclopedic thought and on his political, critical, and constructive teachings. Another chapter concerned the historicity of his thought; his attitude before the religious problem in its connection with the secularizing of the social and political organism (his Jansenism interpreted as "Economicity," sociality, and politics); the coincidences and contrasts between the patriot and the "socialistic" theorist, between the particular national goal and the general moral and civil goal. There is also a chapter "about the vicissitudes of Romagnosianism in Italy" — particularly from 1830 to 1860. Here he follows the contrast of Romagnosianism (in a thousand different aspects) and Catholic idealism (Rosmini), and Mazzinian ethics, in a development of pure thought and practical ends (national *Risorgimento*), and he shows that many events of the Risorgimento—unrelated, apparently—"were in part offspring of Romagnosian *doctrinairism.*"[12] Rebora ends his description by stating that in the appendix he indicates several "nourishing" elements of Romagnosi's thought, especially in relation to Vico, whom he greatly admired.

CHAPTER 5

Teacher

THE STUDY OF ROMAGNOSI NO DOUBT INFLUENCED CLEMENTE Rebora in his choice of a career. As a teacher he was generally successful, and his rapport with students was remarkable, whether in the classroom or elsewhere. He shared his search for Truth with students. Years later, many of them recalled his extraordinary influence, stating that there was an affinity which, at times, caused concern in the students. Rebora too experienced concern.

One day some members of a study group he lectured to, grateful for the inspiring course they had had in 1928, presented Rebora with a beautiful wrought-iron lamp. He, in turn, gave each of them a copy of one of his books which dealt with Indian mysticism. But he soon regretted these gifts, fearing that the contents might be upsetting. He asked that they be destroyed because the book had been published in 1923 with a lengthy commentary and he could no longer judge its merits.

But Rebora's career had not always been marked with success. In fact, his lack of it and sad teaching experiences dated back to 1910 when, as a young teacher, in the midst of the pandemonium raised by his students during their recreation period, he felt frustrated. As he wrote to his friend Daria Malaguzzi: "I have given up and am still giving up, I have sacrificed and I am still sacrificing very much; and sometimes I feel tired like one who has done all he could, without receiving anything in return. . . . I preach well and act badly, you will say: and you are most correct; but this is only one of my numberless defects."[1]

However, four years later, to the same friend, he expressed his love for teaching, stating that his only consolation was finding himself with boys and girls, that with them he was always at home and that, to earn a living, he would want nothing else.[2]

I Substitute Teacher

Upon completing his university studies at the Accademia Scientifico-Letteraria in Milan in 1910, Rebora joyfully related the news to Monteverdi: "With regard to my degree, *alea jacta est*—the die is cast—(today Sunday) with (if the grade interests you) 110/110 and relative honors."[3] He added that, because he had had a very decisive and bitter break with his philology professor, Francesco Novati,[4] he had not expected to pass. The biggest news was that for the past week he had been a substitute, teaching history, geography, and civics *(diritti e doveri)* in a secondary school. He got the appointment through Michele Scherillo,[5] another of his university professors. About his relationship with these professors he wrote: "I no longer understand anything: by dint of being snapped at, they have become kind toward me."[6]

A month later, the tone of his letter to Monteverdi changed—circumstances are such that his "soul is filled with deep sorrow." Fortunately his philosophical spirit still has the power to listen occasionally to the divine voices that give it again "the magnificent bewilderment of the vast quiet of starry infinity." Referring to himself, he says: "I was a professor, I am a private tutor, and I shall be a librarian for about three months, chosen by Scherillo to put in order I don't know which collection of books that belong to the city; and all my energy will be consumed there (from nine a.m. to six-thirty p.m.)."[7]

II Career Frustration

Rebora was subjected to great pressures and overworked. When his colleagues were ready to embark on their careers and continue their studies in Germany, Rebora declared to Nino (Angelo Monteverdi) that he was like a leafless tree. Everything was sterile even though spring announced a thousand invitations to rebirth. With life being so topsy-turvy, he decided to immerse himself in food and put on weight while suffering terribly the loss of his friends. He implored them not to send him any advice, not to try to help him. While he considered all this an exquisite testimony of friendship and affection, they had to realize that he was not a sick man to be cured, but an excellent man to be left alone.[8]

While serving one of the short recalls he was subject to as an ex-soldier, this time from August 12 to September 2, 1910, Rebora lived in horrible quarters and witnessed the ruination of many young men. He had had to face reality in its lowest form, suffering from insect bites and scratches. Back in civilian life, he was considerably annoyed to find a summons to appear in court as a witness in the prosecution of several inveterate ruffians.[9] Other problems affected his peace of mind, bringing about a state of confusion and repeated nervous exhaustion. Envious of his friends—Banfi and Monteverdi—who were accomplishing so much, he refused their invitation to join them in Berlin.[10] He became self-centered, in the solitude of the thundering, crowded city *(questa affollata città rombante),* frequently writing them letters which resounded with expressions that appear in his lyric verses— "I rolled into a dead railroad track" *(ho infilato un binario morto)* —to justify his sentiments.

Up to that point, Rebora had hoped to find a teaching position and join Monteverdi in Rome, but that idea vanished with his friend's departure for Berlin. So he remained in Milan as a substitute instructor while waiting to compete for a government teaching position.

Rebora proctored examinations at a secondary school in Milan, while constantly harboring hopes of teaching there during the new school year. Much to his dismay, the position he hoped for never materialized, and he resigned himself, instead, to taking a substitute-teaching job in Treviglio, a town on the outskirts of Milan, which required him to travel several hours, each day, by train. Although he spent twenty-six hours per week teaching history, geography, and civics, he complained that many hours were wasted in transit, and waiting for classes, and that his finances were also well dissipated by the venture. He no longer had time for music and poetry. "Imagine," he wrote to friend Monteverdi, "the anger and discouragement that is strangling me. I am between Milan and Treviglio, neither here nor there, nauseated with intellectual waste." He then decided to remain a few days a week in Treviglio, since he was becoming broody and it was impossible for him to do anything dear to his heart.

Replying to nostalgic Monteverdi, he reminded him that he was with friends in Berlin and functioning as an apprentice with independence, whereas he found himself alone "in a desert of men, ferociously and brutally missing my friends!"[11]

Rebora's inner voice assured him that he was born to give of himself without receiving anything in return. When daily duties suffocated him the most and around him whirled the victorious mediocrity of numberless egoists, his spirit towered like a giant. He claimed he was forced to give up the most intimate and impelling spiritual activities, with almost all his time given to teaching, which he did with a most precise sense of duty, abandon, and prodigality:

> I feel that I have (and this is what renders teaching so sacred) some creatures for whom I can do some good and whom most people unfortunately consider as "tools of their trade." Not being able to create in my spirit, I attempt to create in life; and it is much more useful that way. I cannot tell you more now, because my most complex soul feels that it is falsifying itself, narrating only here and there certain of its motifs, while its true reality is in the whole symphony of its elements.[12]

At the same time Rebora considered himself an outcast. He was fearful, skeptical, insecure. He was assailed by helplessness and hopelessness, crushed by the knowledge that he could not succeed. He was experiencing the pangs of desperation. Except for several temporary positions in Treviglio and elsewhere, his efforts to obtain a regular teaching position were still unsuccessful. He cursed the "divine power of money," and, again having failed his exams, he rebelled against the school system. One cannot understand what made him fail qualifying exams that less-gifted candidates passed. Rebora was a good, conscientious teacher, yet, in spite of his earnestness and dedication as a substitute in government secondary schools and in spite of his success as a private teacher, he was unable to qualify for a permanent position in the government school system.

The constant frustration, caused by a progressively increasing awareness of being condemned to failure in obtaining the position he most desired, formed the basis of his tragic vision of life during this period.

Rebora's intellectual endowment was far superior to that of the group of examiners who judged of his competency. The poor intellectual quality of these men was a well-known fact which, perhaps, explains his unsuccessful attempts. Students who were not intellectually competent passed the examinations without difficulty. Yet Rebora, who possessed a brilliant mind, was doomed to failure again and again. He deplored the ignorance and inefficiency of his examiners. In May 1911, he again attempted the government competitive exams in order to obtain a teaching position in the normal school's division of secondary schools, that is, that prepared elementary-school teachers. But he withdrew in the middle of the ordeal, overcome by exhaustion. He decided to rest so that he might try with better luck to qualify for some other secondary school. Unexpectedly he was assured a position for one year as a substitute in a local middle school.

Again he resumed his efforts to have a permanent teaching position. Though the preliminary exams were successful, he believed that all his efforts were in vain because so much depended on the attitude of the examiners. He realized he would not be considered suitable because he was not "crafty" enough to qualify. In fact, at the oral examination he violently insulted the examining professors.

All his hopes vanished and, on November 16, he announced the news of his failure. He called the examiners *mafiosi,* meaning thereby that they were Sicilians, or, at any rate, southerners. They treated him with what he felt was premeditated enmity that moved him to insult them angrily. But even if he had passed, his lack of *"seniority"* in the system would have rendered his appointment unlikely. The whole experience brought home to him his absolute ignorance of the ways of the world. While that was humiliating for him, the consciousness he had of his spiritual maturity made him proud enough to consider himself unjustly evaluated. "In other words, while I recognize my present incapacity, I am proud (with a thousand claims) of a potentiality that I detect in myself; that is, I am convinced that were I tomorrow to be entrusted with teaching Italian in a higher institution, I would know how to acquire an adequate culture that would become fruitful life and discipline. And it is because of this conflict that I now kill now exalt myself."[13]

Months earlier he had written practically the same thing to Monteverdi concerning the same competitive examination: "I am a man with a very rich soul, but frightful ignorance; and if I am eliminated, it will be my very own fault." He was tired. The examinations had unnerved him. Treviglio had consumed all his energies in traveling, but what was really causing his prostration was spiritual tension rather than the work he was doing.[14]

Though a failure as an exam taker, he felt at times the urge to "help and elevate everything and everybody; to disappear as a person in order to relive in the best way or in the desire of everyone, be a god who is not seen because he is in the very eyes of the beholder, be an energy that remains unnoticed because it is in the very becoming of every existing thing which is recreated every second."[15]

CHAPTER 6

Friend

REBORA'S MISSION AS A TEACHER WAS NOT LIMITED TO CLASSROOM activity. His letters reveal his interest in serving his friends and his efforts to help solve their problems. When Banfi was in trouble with the Milan Biblioteca Brera for some violation of its rules, he interceded and immediately advised him about what to do next.[1] Later when his friend wanted to teach in the city schools, Rebora instructed him on the procedure to follow, and suggested he come to Milan for better results.[2]

At the age of twenty-seven, Rebora saw in himself the possibility of living the life of "a normal young man," but he rejected it as repugnant to him. He preferred something other than that. He preferred what was "hard, even if unattainable. There is in me, in my innermost being, the keenest sense of reality, of life which is true as panting and hammering of every single minute and every single thing: and I feel remorse—even though beyond my power—for not realizing every divine minute. For me, even the most mediocre daily patch-up job is a rapture: but as I understand it intellectually, I hate it in the emotion that would like something else. I toss in the contrast between the eternal and the transitory, between what I feel (and love) necessary and what I wish were not, between the potential and the actual."[3]

Following his teaching career, one must note Rebora's literary endeavors. One cannot date his early poetry, which no doubt required years of retouching and revision. They are lyric fragments of a truly restless spirit, a self-questioning individual, never at peace with himself, never quite satisfied with his accomplishments. References in his letters express these sentiments, moods, and attitudes which are also found in the poetry of this same period.

During this period too is the struggle for the publication of his lyric fragments. Once, afraid to give a premature comment on his own poetry, which had a certain affinity with Cesarina Rossi's, Rebora preferred not to judge her book of poems. When he was asked for a recommendation and book review of her *Senza Approdo* (Without a landing-place), he remarked: "They are not *poems,* but, by God, is there poetry!"[4] The following day he sent the book to Prezzolini, saying that it was worthy "of being taken into consideration."[5] When Prezzolini asked about the author, he explained that she was the daughter of a rich lawyer, an ex-student of the Accademia Scientifico-Letteraria who failed to receive her degree several years before, perhaps because of her contemptuous attitude at school. He remembered her as a companion who among companions was considered always "senza approdo."[6] He asked his friend Monteverdi to review the book publicly, while he, always honest with his friends, proceeded to do so privately in a letter to her, with both favorable and unfavorable comments.[7]

In 1912, aware of marital difficulties his friend Daria was having, he encouraged her to return to Milan and continue her studies at the university. He realized that there would be repercussions about her decision to leave her husband for Antonio Banfi and feared for her future, since divorce was not recognized in Italy. He realized too that she and Banfi needed his moral support: and so he gave her that of the "purified" friendship he felt for her and Banfi—an intense friendship that "is something resting on the very reason for the destiny and the mysterious inner affinities, besides affection and esteem; and I like to shout it out right now, when a certain immoral morality of certain right-thinking people could—and will—judge wrongly. Yet few are so Mazzinianly rigid as I!"[8]

When Daria and Banfi decided about their "union," Rebora was entrusted with the task of notifying their mutual friends. He asked them to accept the news with the warm profound humanity which it deserved. Their friends were all in accord and pleased to know of the couple's happiness. In a letter to Angelo Monteverdi, Rebora, speaking of the love "fatefully and divinely flared up" between the two, added: "It was both a sad and a joyful thing, a necessity surfacing on their destiny which gradually and unavoidably took hold of all the emotions of their lives, up to the heroic decision to sanctify in their union the marvelous law that caused them to gravitate toward each other;

heroic, if you consider the dangers to which they expose their own security and practical respectability, and how unkind is the world of mankind toward those who select a holy and true morality, but so unusual and contrasting with tradition whether good or the triumph of a brutal hypocrisy."[9]

I State of Mind

The contrasting, contradictory statements one finds in Rebora's letters very frequently reveal his spiritual state of mind, as in one to Daria in which he says that there were moments when it seemed to him that "to live is to harm someone, just as anyone walking kills with each step some infinitesimal living thing; one would want to do so much good, and instead one harms himself and others."[10]

And to Banfi: "All that moves me during the day (from some inadequacy in my job to the news of the [Tripoli] war, to a little phrase in a book, to a very slight misunderstanding with a dear person, etc.) is a large part in the work of nutrition on the one hand and, on the other, of the dissolution of me as a practical and thinking man. . . . My God, I am in a period in which I detest refined, difficult, complex, literary introspection, and when I speak—even to you which is tantamount to speaking to myself—I get entangled and struggle so!"[11]

He had already told Banfi that his fine body prospered in atrocious and incomprehensible contrast to the mental ills that afflicted him, due to numberless and inexpressible causes. "Besides," he wrote, "I have such pride of virility—even in the midst of total shipwreck—that forbids or embitters my confessing and calling for help: also because I feel its uselessness. . . ." Rebora denied his condition when others told him he was dangerously depressed, stating: "Now, in me subsist and will continue to subsist permanent reasons for the impossibility of 'living'—strange, isn't it, in this handsome young man who in the army, naked before doctors, was gazed upon as a fine specimen of the race!"[12]

Rebora was ever ready to bemoan his lack of "knowledge," both practical and scientific, a lack which if, he thought, he had had the courage to reveal it to his friends, they would have considered him "a mere street cleaner." He asked them to leave him in his miseries to rot (or to be reborn). Yet it would have been hell for him to lose the esteem of his friends. He recognized that the only virtue which remained firm in him, in fact more pertinacious and solid than ever, was his "goodness."

II *Missionary Spirit*

His goodness triumphed, and at that time, his missionary spirit revealed itself. He wished to dedicate himself to the rural population in Calabria as a teacher and confessed to his friend Daria: "I wasted my little treasure years ago and there are obstacles—independent of my will—that forbid its recovery; to this add an almost total loss of strength under the appearance of florid and tenacious health."[13] He explained that he was in communication with political leaders—Tommaso Gallarati Scotti and Umberto Zanotti Bianco—who were responsible for this experiment in Reggio Calabria. He hoped to begin living there on his earnings in October, dedicating himself in his free time to the work of the cultural orientation and the moral regeneration of southern Italy, under the sponsorship of the National Association for the Mezzogiorno (The South). In this way he hoped to show his "love of Italy." But after informing his friends and family of his plans, nothing materialized for him and he was obliged to remain in Milan.

Rebora needed the reassurance and acceptance of his friends. Never had he felt so fragmented while longing to appear whole. He became arrogant because insecure. He craved for praise and recognition, yet scorned them when given. Yet he wished ardently for companionship. Fortunately, his association with Giuseppe Prezzolini opened the way for him to join the writers of *La Voce*.

Although Rebora's contributions to *La Voce* were few in number and limited to the years 1913-15, his correspondence with Prezzolini goes back to early 1909. *La Voce* had just appeared, and Rebora hastened to express to its founder his cordial approbation and support. In April of 1911 they finally met in Florence, and the attraction which already existed between them became friendship. On his return home, he wrote to Daria: "What profound emotions! Here I met and sympathized with Prezzolini . . . who is the standardbearer of a moral and practical rebirth announced at the dawn of the twentieth century, which will take its place in history as the preparation of a vaster renaissance of mankind and God."[14]

CHAPTER 7

La Voce *Movement*

La Voce (1908 - 1914) WAS A PERIODICAL DEDICATED TO THE moral, social, and intellectual regeneration of Italy. Its founder and first editor, Giuseppe Prezzolini,[1] became the moving spirit behind a whole generation of writers known as *vociani*. *La Voce* thus became the rallying point of many of the best minds of the Italy of those days, minds of all shades of political thought and religious belief, united only by their common desire to promote a spiritual regeneration.

Besides this periodical, Prezzolini also founded, in 1910, the *Libreria della Voce*, a publishing house that made known not only some of the best works of the younger generation of Italian writers, but also some of the best contemporary European writers.

Part of the intricate and convulsive moments of the literary renewal by the *vociani* were works by Giovanni Papini, Scipio Slataper, Renato Serra, Piero Jahier, Ardengo Soffici, Camillo Sbarbaro, and Clemente Rebora.[2] Contributors to *La Voce* were such outstanding writers as Benedetto Croce, Giovanni Gentile, Luigi Ambrosini, Giovanni Amendola, and Emilio Cecchi, as well as Gaetano Salvemini, Romolo Murri, and Giovanni Boine. Their contributions did not deal exclusively with the arts and literature but also with music, philosophy, economics, religion, and politics. These writers had a deep awareness of social and spiritual issues. Their credo was action.

I *Giuseppe Prezzolini*

Clemente Rebora was extremely proud of his friendship with Prezzolini. To Angelo Monteverdi he wrote that it was both "lively and cordial" and that the editor of *La Voce* was a "young man who—on meeting him—can be judged only with affection, attraction, esteem as the criterion."[3] He stated too that, as a result, he had been sought out by the old collaborators of *Il Rinnovamento*,[4] and also by the political leader Giovanni Amendola.[5] He was pleased to be among the contributors to *La Voce*. Moreover, the editor had faith in him and encouraged him to publish his poetry in 1913. He speaks of his first poetic volume—*Frammenti lirici*—in his autobiographical poem, *Curriculum Vitae*. It is a vivid, personal, and significant interpretation of his early years:

> In the civil asphyxia,
> while the devil plotted his havoc,
> I, held in the Ego's claw,
> bundled up Wisdom from all races
> to elude Learning:
> and meantime what crumbling!
> Not like fibers fused into one single trunk
> were my thoughts, but a bundle of twigs
> which upon coming untied revert each to itself.
> When dying seemed to me the only escape,
> singing was for me a passage of air to breathe:
> poetry led to truth.
> But not every song is a good breath;
> nor do all verses make poetry.

II La Voce *Articles*

During this period other poems appeared in *La Voce* and in the *Almanacco della Voce*. There were also several articles, the first being a review of Alfredo Panzini's *Manualetto di rettorica*, with the title: "The Rhetoric of a Humorist." *(La rettorica di un umorista)*.[6] Rebora considered this text "a work of art, in its own right," capable of helping professors willing to work "in their efforts to revitalize their classes." The last of the four articles written for *La Voce* was a review of another book by the same author: "Simple Elements of Italian Grammar" *(Semplici nozioni di grammatica italiana)*.[7] He expressed gratitude for the work, which revealed where the essentials of grammar lie, and endeavored to solve the difficulties teachers find in teaching grammar. He hoped schools would be aware of it, but unfortunately, he added ironically, "they are not aware and perhaps will not be for some time."

Rebora's attraction to Panzini, one of the best contemporary writers, continued throughout his life. They resembled each other in several ways: both were remarkable educators, yet unable to obtain government teaching positions; both were intelligent and sincere writers whose works during that period were recognized only by the group of *La Voce*.

Panzini, in his *Sentimental Diary of the War* (*Diario sentimentale della guerra*),[8] records his visit to Rebora in the war zone. He speaks of him as a former professor, philosopher, and poet who adored Nietzsche, the German philosopher and poet (his memory must have played him false!); now turned infantry sergeant but aspiring to join the Alpine Corps, the army group he considered the best weapon of Italy. In answer to Panzini's questions about "pure poetry," the poet remarked that "poetry should be free from all references to any other value: without doctrinal content, a pure act, a creative moment," not particularly an original idea in the days of Benedetto Croce.

Rebora accompanied his article "Goodness, Boys, and *La Voce* (Answer to no question)" [*Bontà, ragazzi e "Voce" (Risposta a nessuna domanda)*] with a letter to Prezzolini hoping his answer would neither displease nor surprise him. He admired the editor's freedom-of-the-press policy observed in *La Voce*, which constituted one of its greatest merits. The article was to be a proof of their mutual affection and independence.

It was published on May 8, 1913, and criticized those acquiring middle-class status who think they have found the solution to the harassing problems of life by renouncing their ideals. Ironically he wrote: "Oh, to feel like *good boys,* modest, respectful, inconclusive, without hope of absolution from mankind, or from the universe that keeps the records, or from the conscience that it gave us and will want back with interest; to feel useless with the eternal torment of not ever being anything except being of good will. . . ."[9] In the same article, he found fault with the school where he taught—its academic program, its faculty, its method of instruction. "Little knowledge is transmitted," he wrote, "because everywhere there are obstacles and lack of understanding." Soon after, he was making another effort to correct the system in "Life that goes to School and Vice Versa" *(La vita che va a scuola e viceversa).*[10]

III Spiritual Search

It was in this atmosphere of *La Voce* that Rebora decided to reveal in verse his personal drama—the first part of his spiritual search. At times bitter, at times violent, *Frammenti lirici* (1913) is marked by a striking sincerity, and it is here that we find Rebora's more human poetry. Years later he stated: "Poetry was an outlet for me in the bitter desperation caused by the lack of God. It helped me and instilled in me a longing for truth."[11]

Because of his preoccupation with things moral, Rebora's poetry had an almost "religious" aspect. He never identified himself with the poets of *La Voce*. He was not ironical like Aldo Palazzeschi, egocentric like Umberto Saba, skeptical like Camillo Sbarbaro. For a time he may have felt an affinity with Jahier insofar as he had the same humanitarian aspirations and the same compassion for humble people. Rebora admired the courageous innovations of other contributors to *La Voce,* such as Prezzolini and Papini, whom he loved dearly, but whose views he did not always share. The only writer—who could also be called a poet—for whom Rebora felt a spiritual kinship and from whom he received comprehension and praise was Boine, who had been a fellow student at the Accademia Scientifico-Letteraria of Milan. He had thought highly of him and had recommended him to Papini as willing and able to contribute a volume on Romagnosi to Papini's collection of annotated classics, *Cultura dell'anima*. Rebora and Boine both possessed sensitive natures and lived similar tormented lives. It was to Boine that Rebora wrote: ". . . you are one of the very few that I feel near in my moments of strength. I am really very fond of you."[12]

In the September 1914 issue of *Riviera Ligure,* speaking of Rebora's poetry, Boine finds that it is vigorously traditional in its feeling and rhythm, that it is truly Italian as is the poetry of Dante, Michelangelo, Tommaso Campanella, Giordano Bruno, Leopardi. Overcome by its effect on him he concludes that it is *"Grande."*

IV Self-Criticism

It was not Rebora's opinion of his own poems. He constantly revised and rearranged his verses. For years he was undecided as to whether or not he should publish them. Either he wanted his friends to burn those they were reading or suggested that they comment or help him search for a publisher. In fact, he appealed to his friend Monteverdi to find out what it would cost to publish about two hundred pages of verse.

While considering himself a lyricist, he did not dare call himself a poet. Indeed, in rereading his verses he was "nauseated." Because of his many duties, he did not have the time to dress his poetic offspring decently. He felt that perhaps he was deceiving himself about their right to life, since old or new, serious or ephemeral, they were all equally unsuitable, and belonged to the previous decade.[13]

Rebora lived his poetry. At the time of the *Frammenti lirici* he was searching for the real meaning of life, a purpose for human actions, a higher motive for living and acting in a world that seemed hopelessly chaotic. At first he was groping for an immanent security, later a transcendent one. For him, in the words of his brother Piero, "Poetry should be love, dedication, fruitful action, an introduction to *goodness,* which was for him a higher ideal of human redemption. Men *are* when they love and devote themselves to goodness, which is the supreme truth."[14]

Rebora was associated with the *vociani* during this period but "without ever betraying his commitment, his faith, that is, without reducing or attenuating the intensity of his ideas. It is difficult to explain his poetry in terms of the fads, the practices and the tendencies of his times."[15]

For Rebora, as for other *vociani,* the aesthetic revolution had a predominantly moral meaning. In seeking new ideas and new answers, their themes were relevant, as they tried to understand society. They all shared common metaphysical concerns. Jahier in *Radiocorriere*[16] declared that Rebora's "polemical burden forms part of a more profound discourse, is in the service of that spiritual cast which constitutes the true innovation brought by Rebora into the literary panorama of twentieth-century Italy."

CHAPTER 8

Frammenti lirici

THE UNDERLYING IDEA OF THE FIRST POEM IN *Frammenti lirici,* "Life ever the same and diverse presses about" *(L'egual vita diversa urge intorno),* does not come as a surprise. Rebora seems to say that the only way to solve the problem of life is to live it worthily, that is, to make it easier for others to live.

In the first part of the poem, he confesses a dissatisfaction with life, which he depicts as one long monotony even in its variations, an indecipherable enigma: "Life ever the same and diverse presses about;/ I seek but do not find, therefore set forth/ in its unending motion." Apparently, one may drift along with it: living may seem routine, but to the thoughtful it is instinct with a terrifying mystery: "To follow it seems custom or chance,/ but inside it strikes fear." It would be desirable to unravel this mystery, to pierce the intense darkness within. Unlike Leonardo, who experienced fear and desire at the mouth of the cavern, "Fear of the dark threatening cavern, desire to see whether there might be any marvelous thing therein,"[1] Rebora was dominated more by fear than desire. He concludes that the wisest thing to do is just to go on living, without seeking an explanation:

> He loses the irrevocable present
> who scrutinizes it;
> the iron ticking of the hour allows
> neither mellifluous abandon
> nor oblivious enchantment.

It is here that Rebora has his lyric invocation to time. Time means man's destiny, his life; and all attempts to grasp and to understand it are doomed to fail. *"Sirena del tempo,"* he calls it—a siren that lures and tantalizes but never surrenders.

And when I leap to embrace you
—Siren of time—
barely a bite and a lock of hair do I get from you:
or else, uncaught, you flee, and without a scream
I kill you in my mind
and drown in the act.

I *Giacomo Leopardi*

The siren's bite, that is, sorrow and disappointment, and her lock, that is, the little that he can wrest from her slippery person, are perhaps good as a memento for Rebora, but signify nothing substantial. One thinks of Leopardi's pleasurable immersion in thoughts of infinity, losing himself to limitless spaces in the *"Infinito,"* where his fancy so strongly works that his "heart is almost frightened." But Rebora's drowning is the discomfiture of an activist whose strength—rare indeed during this period—may be traced to forgetfulness of self, to suffering the effects of working so profoundly, almost wishing to dissolve himself into a sensually mystical frenzy. For him, the moment is terribly and sadly divine; for him, thought and abstraction do not exist. He has constant remorse, and it is difficult for him to accomplish what he wants.[2]

Rebora craved for infinity. On February 12, 1912, he wrote to Antonio Banfi:

What you experience, perhaps I have already experienced and—not infrequently—still do. And the cause of it is in part an effort to root us to our *natura naturans;* a determining of values, in the clash of the *certain*—of a reason infinitely necessary of transmutability—with the *true* that flashes inside and thus justifies itself and exalts itself and assumes new positions. And in the contrasting lyricism—but not contradicting itself—of joy and sorrow; the *eternal vanity* of thinking like a spindle that spins, pulling the distant strings into a large ball that changes itself into a burst of creation; in a love of the moment endured and refilled to the utmost; in a crude concreteness of so-called matter and in self-abandon as well in the why and the how of ourselves and the world, not abstract, but just in this place here, with this tendency, with this irresolute desire or that irresolvable wish, that colors, intones, in quite the same specific way all our reality. In short—at least for me . . . when I am . . . myself . . . the divinization of the moment, which is a terrible tactile thing and at the same time an infinity that remains while transmuting.[3]

Frammenti lirici

In the second part of the poem, the poet tries to forget himself and his pessimism. He becomes less personal, more social-minded. He wants to give of himself to others. It is his dream to take and to give:

> Even though the eternal is my trunk,
> history my foliage and homeland my flower,
> still I would fain pour forth my sap
> from the root into the vivid whole
> and with happy alternating vigor
> suck in the sunshine and lavish the fruit;
> I would have my heart reveal
> by its rhythm human destiny
> and have you, clear-sighted
> passion for the world,
> fair, sturdy goodness,
> become the air breathed
> by him who treads on locked up in his toil.
> Here is born, here dies my song;
> and maybe it will seem a vain
> solitary chord.

In the closing lines, Rebora successfully employs the somewhat archaic envoy of the Provençal tradition: "But you who are listening, take it/ to your good and to your ill:/ and you will find it obscure." In both content and form *"L'egual vita diversa urge intorno"* is typical of the young Rebora.

II Basic Questions of Life

The themes of the first poem of *Frammenti lirici* recur, though in elaborated form— "In the blue evening darkness" *(Nella seral turchina oscurità)*.

> In the blue evening darkness
> the plain vaporing peace over snow
> broadens out melodiously;
> time ever the same is like a brook
> that seems not to flow,
> and the universe reveals itself artlessly
> as the child to its mother, when she is alone.

Again the poet raises the basic question of life's meaning and purpose. Shall we be satisfied with a superficial reading of the universe that does not go beyond shallow delights and childish daydreams? Or must we probe beneath the beautiful appearances in search of another reality, and work for its realization in our own life and that of others? Or is it possible to reconcile both the dream and the action? The temptation to watch life go by, to let the river of time run quietly away, while standing alone on a lonely shore, is a great temptation. Nature can be so beautiful: the blue of the evenings, the snow, the lovely feeling of communion with creatures when they seem to bare themselves to our understanding *"come alla mamma, quando è sola, il bimbo"* (as does the child to its mother when she is alone). There is something of an intoxication in this passive contemplation, in this surrender to the belief that we are part of the universe, in this infinite togetherness with the whole that becomes almost ecstatic.

> I am the life of each created thing
> and caresses tremble in my hands
> and an inviting glance
> blossoms in my eyes:
> my heart is blissfully a rapture
> of boundless rapport
> and rising from nature indistinct
> mystery becomes a passion
> in which the world courses.
> You were and are my desire
> which changed its facets
> but never its God;
> you who were an intimation renewing
> secret reality,
> barely touching which, you fled farther away;
> you who were thought
> and wished to lavish
> its invisible powers,
> unbridled riderless mares from battle
> pantingly foaming from the fray;
> you who were music
> —Goddess friend, not lover—
> and made tuneful my pulse beats,
> but the rhythm you locked inside
> throwing off lethargy:

Frammenti lirici 55

> you who were much else
> and the more divine the more concrete.

At the same time man has a vital urge to be creative, a strange, strong, irrepressible urge *(impeto strano)* to work toward some worthy goal:

> Creative urge,
> why do you become so hard-incrusted
> in urban developments,
> or else less translucid glow
> or dolefully sink low?
> What is it you are doing if not employing
> this boundless dream of yours where life abides?
> And yet here is tested
> sublime destiny;
> mere, vibrant goodness,
> you who pursue the eternal
> in the fleeting day.
> Mother, sod air light,
> father, trunk pure and stern,
> brothers, my branches and my nest,
> sisters, my leaves and my buds,
> O good blood of ours sweet
> to see and to sip,
> while I would want to love
> and helpfully lose myself in you,
> I don't know you, I don't crown you
> in the hour that comes and vanishes
> postponing all communion to a later date.
> Strange urge, be strong
> under time's yoke; and relive
> your faith in the deed,
> like him who sees no light
> while it shines upon rapt labors.
> Heedless shy dreams,
> here we fight and die:
> the idea is in the doing.

The poet has made his choice, at least momentarily. Let us work now, he says, and postpone *"i consensi più in là!"* Time may seem to stand still but the fleeting day has value only when the best in us *(fremente bontà)* seeks what is lasting, eternal *(l'eterno insegui)*. No matter how close we may feel to the pretty things of nature and how familiarly we address them *(mamma, papà, fratelli, sorelle),* they must be ignored and forgotten. Action is of the essence, though even while absorbed in it, man does not see any light. That is, he does not find the perfect explanation of our *sublime destiny:* "Like him who sees no light/ while it shines upon rapt labors." But the work man is doing is full of light and that is enough. Away, then, "Heedless shy dreams,/ here we fight and die:/ the idea is in the doing." This is Idealism with a Mazzinian flavor; it is the ideal common to the group of *La Voce.* Stylistically the poem mirrors the conflicts within the poet. When he is lost in the contemplation of nature, the verses have a quiet, unbroken flow. They glide. When he is wrestling with his own problems, the verse becomes suddenly hard, the lyrical flow is arrested like streaming water over rocks. Particular attention should be called to some beautiful lines (that is, the first thirteen) and to images so exclusively Rebora's own, like *"e melodiavi i bàttiti dei polsi"* (and made melodies of the pulse beats), and the entire litany addressed to the various elements—sod, air, light, trunk, branches, nest, leaves, buds *(zolla, aria, luce, tronco, rami, nido, foglie, gemme).* The pace of the poem is swift and vigorous. It contains urgency, passion, and, above all, a moving sincerity.

III *Poetic Inspiration*

Not only in content but also in form and in vocabulary, Rebora's early poetry reflected, at times, the theories and intellectual movements then in vogue. He was inspired by both Mazzinianism and Idealism. There are passages which recall Vico in the poem "Through the acrid flow of the minutes" *(Per l'acre fluir dei minuti):*

> The idea dallies around the bends
> and, rushing out, frightens me.
> It puts on my flesh and hides
> fingered by a dream of nightmares,
> it waves nerves for lace and fibrils
> of veins for hair,
> it stares in the face with wide-open pupils
> red from a broken heart;
> but the usual hand
> gives me all where I abide.

Frammenti lirici

> However, if the minute does not find
> its groove and eddies,
> —as seaweed lost in a current,
> while loitering in some inlet
> gathers refuse and foam—
> the copies of the world, which before
> were joy and sorrow
> through the sequel of time,
> crowd in the middle and back
> comes their weight with dead breath:
> the minute eddies and back
> comes the idea with dead breath,
> the idea that on coming back
> drags along a fact; and forever.

One notes in this poem that the common idiom does not suffice for Rebora. He does not hesitate to use farfetched, figurative language in order to make his poetry more vivid and original:

> In my breath and blood an idea
> chokes me without cries
> consumes me without flame
> whether I sleep, prepare, toil,
> talk, or devour my meal:
> but the usual hand
> gives me all where I abide.
> The contrast in man, the world, God
> roars, shines, is inspired;
> and I taste and sprinkle myself at the various
> perennial fountain that seems
> a thing but is spirit and heaven,
> that seems the infinite but is lymph
> of the day sprinkling in the motions and utterances
> of intense unremitting activity.

Among classical references and echoes of modern poets, there are references and passages that recall Dante. But the context is typically Reborian, as in "Wasted Days" *(Giorni dispersi):*

> O mighty for human progress
> ineluctable certainty of truth
> weave, weave your threads into the cloth

> which in its texture is solidly history
> and in its pattern is eternally God.

Or in "Suffering" *(Soffrire):*

> And I do not want you, O few wise men
> of the immortal round,
> to be more alive than my silly flesh;
> I thought anyone sorrowing without hope
> would die by nature,
> but on my dry soul ripe pulp
> grows spitefully more beautiful!
> Let me be . . .
> Terse vigor of welling water,
> quiet of tranquil laughter,
> sated blandishment of the senses,
> an ephemeral thing of time
> among ephemeral things.

The sonnet "Defeat" *(Sconfitta)* bemoans the triumph of evil:

> While I chisel in deafened custom
> blow by blow the passing of days
> distrustfully I live on hope
> that this age will prove fruitful to me;
>
> or if with tenacity I boldly mine a passage
> for others and myself, on failing
> I plunge down amid jeers, and a blind distance
> isolates me within rugged surroundings;
>
> or if full of joy up from its afflicted lair
> the holiness of the world in contrast
> reveals to me the greatest truth enthralling it,
>
> upon returning among the people I am defeated;
> again I take in the blows, groan under the yoke:
> Christ is right but Machiavelli triumphs.

Rebora's poetry reflects the expectancy, the awareness, the desire for the supernatural, as expressed in the final lines of "Suffering":

Frammenti lirici

> Let me be . . .
> an ephemeral thing of time
> among ephemeral things:
> but in the tripping of the little foot
> hear the divine step,
> a silent guide to the believer.

Even when Rebora does not speak expressly of God, he senses or intimates His presence. Through poetic intuition Rebora succeeds in resolving the conflict between human life (how men live, think, act, suffer) and nature (lakes, mountains, stars, all that reflects a superior force). There is a profound need for communion with nature and a tormenting anxiety to reach reality:

> Now, like the blood here in me,
> necessary and tortuous
> I am within life;
> unsurely the heaped up past
> weighs upon the memory,
> but neatly the present wedges into its merciless place
> with dread and sorrow
> in hated sleep the only deception.
> But, a gorge at a sudden mountain turn,
> the awakening seems a dreadful ambush
> where anxiety and the future
> lay down an unavoidable barrage of threats,
> relentlessly demand answers,
> while it is dismay to hear all around
> the day again rousing to toil.
> Like an arrow gripped in light by the air,
> O reality, would I like to be in you:
> but in a concrete and alternating
> change I lose the meaning
> of your eternal vortex.

IV *Pessimism*

It is in this lyric "Suffering" that Rebora manifests his pessimistic concept of life both in thought and in form which recall Leopardi's poem *"A Silvia"* and his *"Weltschmerz"* (World-sorrow). Leopardi saw in life only evil and death, the end of that which should not have been born. Not so with Rebora, who saw himself as spirit in as yet a pantheistic conception of the universe:

> Tragically the idea, which where it ranges
> contains the all within, and nature
> which creates without me, come into contrast.
> Why is suffering sure
> and understanding obscure?
> Why does open and cheerful desire
> miserably go under?
> That is not as you promised, O childhood!

Rebora's reference to his lost youth recalls Leopardi's intensely personal grief in *"A Silvia,"* where, in his bitter reproach to Nature he includes all humanity: "O Nature, O Nature,/ why do you not then give us/ what you promised when we were young?/ Why do you deceive your children so?" *(O natura, o natura,/ Perchè non rendi poi/ Quel che prometti allor? perchè di tanto/ Inganni i figli tuoi?).*

Asked in 1913 whether he felt affinity with Carducci, D'Annunzio, or Pascoli, Rebora said that if there was anyone he felt it with, it was Leopardi, on whom as a student he had written his minor thesis—an essay on music entitled *"Per un Leopardi mal noto,"* an analysis of harmony and sound in Leopardi's work. It became his first publication, appearing in the September 1910 issue of the *Rivista d'Italia.*

Rebora refers to past joys and sorrows, to his dreams and raptures:

> When I was barely footsteps or rest
> in the wind of my meadow;
> when I tastefully sipped living,
> unconscious and eager as my palate;
> when the aroma of my dreams wafted
> from the glowing corolla of my senses
> to the shining presage of rapture,
> Oh attraction of joy
> Oh creation of a world
> that now I pursue vainly and shun,
> that makes me what I am not
> and farthest away where I pine most!

Frammenti lirici

Filled with nostalgia, he adds, apostrophizing reality:

> Born of you [reality] hollow, I fade away,
> (vapor over water in wintertime):
> and to realize as much hurts, and I refuse
> your awesome offer.

As in Leopardi, nostalgia took hold of Rebora. He recalled the emotions of his youthful years that might have been sweet had he possessed faith and hope. Suffering, disillusion, and melancholy were themes that surged in his soul when he was surrounded by the harsh realities of life and bitter contacts with society.

Unlike Leopardi, Rebora expressed a deep sense of the eternal. He would like to feel that which is divine in everything. He would like to hear "the divine step" *(il passo divino)*, which he calls "a silent guide to the believer" *(tacita guida a chi crede)*.

V *"Canto di Donna"* and Other Lyric Fragments

There are lyrical fragments in Rebora's work which cannot be forgotten, such as "A Woman's Song" *(Canto di donna)*, a spontaneous poem, truly original in its clarity and its lament of a beauty vanishing without love, compared to a spark that fails to become a flash, a vital plant uprooted, a firebrand forgotten under the flue:

> A woman's long song filters
> like blue vapor
> from the slopes skimmed by the autumn sun
> tiredly thinning out the heat of the leaves
> and melting slumber-seeking clouds.
> In the empty tarrying of the listening air
> her voice throbs in my heart:
> and I think again of her charms
> that lonely vanish without love:
> a golden spark not turned to flash,
> a vital plant uprooted, a firebrand
> forgotten under the flue
> to dream of flame,
> a breath unbreathed,
> kisses unopened,
> a sturdy body without embrace.

From the slopes pours down, exhales, despairs
the damp purple shadowing:
back home, to squeeze the evening!

Another poem of this type is "Summer Evening" *(Sera estiva),* in which the poet expresses sentiments both of a critical-reflective nature filled with severe moralism, and of a lyrical-musical nature rich with psychological movements and secret melancholy. The last lines are truly Carduccian: "O tired of dreaming, sleep today:/ all, tomorrow, will begin again" *(O stanchi di sognar, oggi dormite: tutto, domani, ricomincerà).*

The dissatisfaction and restlessness characteristic of Rebora's early life are also eloquently manifested in another lyric, "O sidetracked empty car" *(O carro vuoto sul binario morto).* The poet first pictures man as destined to an earthly life of uncontrolled impulses, of unsatisfied longing, of suppressed freedom of soul. He employs the analogy of a freight car waiting on a sidetrack, jolted to and fro by the movements of the other cars. Then, attached to the engine, it is burdened with merchandise, "on the taut frames" *(sui telai tesi),* one of the many cars that will form the train. There follows a brief, vivid description of the bellowing monster that advances toward its prey:

> O sidetracked empty car
> here comes your rough freight of bumps
> and thumps. Heavy-laden now you weigh
> on the taut frames;
> but with swollen groans
> the smoke-belching engine rocks
> and comes sniffing with horrid charm
> to take you in tow.
> Away you go from your self-collected spot
> to the rough rumbling of steel,
> to the jolting screeching of brakes,
> chained in the herd
> by the changeless law
> of the endless open road:
> and rolling in tow you pass on
> and standing still you hold back
> your untold secret power
> over the wheels close by
> and the never-to-meet downtrodden rails,

>   under the sky that erratically
>   in the maze of the days
>   at the crossroads of the seasons
>   unleashes the eternal against boredom,
>   opens toward love a vast expanse,
>   and dies not, much as it would, and lives not, as it would,
>   while earth asks for its word
>   and passionate in her bitter wish
>   pays with her blood, alone, for her faith.

For Carducci the train was a manifestation of Satan,[4] that is, of the spirit of progress. But where Carducci sees progress, Rebora sees a monstrous and monotonous fatality. Once coupled to the engine, the car is also joined to the others. In this way it goes on and on, at the mercy of their movement and of the frequent dictates of the brakes. And even in this, man, a prisoner of a capricious destiny, resembles the empty car. But the poet refuses to stop at the concept of life, which is full of boredom and absurdity. He heeds the call to a higher and eternal life and manages to catch a glimpse of the infinite sky.

VI *The Fever of Life*

Rebora's life was a simple one, lived amid the noise of dynamic Milan, the most modern industrial city of Italy, ringed by the peaceful majestic Alps and enveloped in the silence of the great lakes of Italy—Como, Maggiore, Garda. It was here, against the two contrasting backdrops of man's feverish activities and the immense peace of nature's mountains and waters, amid unknown and uncaring crowds and a small, intimate group of chosen friends, that Rebora grew from childhood to adolescence, to manhood, to literary activities, to trench life, to vague uncertain mysticism, to faith and certainty. Indeed, much of this growth, to be rightly understood, has to be viewed against the background of the smart, though boisterous, city, the Alpine splendor and the blue sky of northern Italy, and the swaying of palm trees on lake shores gently swept by almost imperceptible waves.

For Rebora, nature represented the mystery of the universe, the infinite, God. But in contrast with nature, which is good and pure, Milan became, with its deafening industrial clamor, a symbol of anguish and inquietude. Rebora saw only a modern

Milan: he did not notice any of its antiquity, its history, its literature. Nor did he see its cathedral, its old churches and monuments, the intellectual and moral characteristics of the Milanese. Nothing else existed for Rebora: he saw only factories, commerce, smoke, and the movement of crowds.

This atmosphere was also reflected in his letters, when he speaks of the "voracious city," the "crowded, boisterous city," the "lustful city without love."

In his poetry, Rebora paints a picture of the "city" and is able "to hear" the train in "Ever farther on" *(Sempre più in là):*

> The train whistles and slides lividly along
> in a pool of smoke and air
> which spills convulsively.
> Beyond the haze,
> dripping rows of plants run through fields and ditches,
> and swerve in the distance, grief-stricken:
> hamlets and hovels find their bearings,
> and spin submerged in their lair;
> but from the depth
> veiled distance watches and withdraws.
> From the windows my eye roams,
> and a great sense expands in the rhythm.

Frequently Rebora's agitation and dissatisfaction with life are expressed by trying to intensify the ideas that are dear to him. To achieve this he makes use of the repetition of words or phrases:

> Oh, how the things I view do change,
> and I would like to have them!
> Oh, how the life I feel does change,
> and I would like to have it!
> What is near me,
> wrapped in itself does not incite me:
> the inexplicable moment
> is a specter in between;
> what beckons me from afar,
> goes ever farther on:
> and nothing exists as I pass by.

From the tumult of the "city," Rebora takes refuge in the peace of the Alps, and he turns to writing an idyll, though with

Frammenti lirici

less effectiveness. "Nocturnal Chorale" *(Corale notturno)* is the description of the mountain folk he so often observed. It is late evening. The great song of the night—human voices and the noise of the waters below—has begun. It reaches and circles the stables where the folk have retired after the day's work:

> With the selfsame stir of your people, O valley,
> from the dark, reverberating din
> the nocturnal chorale
> rises lullabylike up the mountainsides,
> and reeks of shadows at the nest of stables.

In a humble hut, a group of people are gathered around the fire. The coals burn bright and low, casting strange lights and shadows. One sees dark features almost bent upon the fire; one sees clear, sparkling eyes; one hears the sound of prayers. The mountain folk pray quietly and earnestly, like children telling fascinating tales. Finally all is silent; all are asleep. Even the fire goes out with a last flash. The vast sky watches over the pastoral scene, filtering through a hole in the roof, as if from a needle's eye:

> Here, in the den there stoops
> amid the shifting of embers
> the rude, famished form
> of the gathered kin,
> light-eyed and dark-faced;
> and there wafts through the air the sound of Hail Mary's
> almost like the quiet chatter of children
> when busy swapping fibs.
> Then quietly every one is resting,
> and with a last flicker the fire too undresses.
> The sky filters in and keeps watch through a cranny.

Only one man is awake. And now he has gone outside. He is restless. On the threshold of the hut he looks and listens. The mountains make a circle around him in the damp night. They too look and listen in their quiet way. The poet contrasts his feelings of agitation with the calm of the sleeping mountaineers. They are simple men of good will who work and pray and rest. And that is why, muses the poet, they merit the visit and the kiss of the angel that mysteriously walks the earth at night:

> Silent on the threshold,
> eye and ear I strain
> through the humid round of mountains;
> and if to my strange musings I compare
> these motionless humble forms
> lying indoors, a mysterious
> phantom issues from the earth
> and kisses only those asleep.

"The Last Trill" *(L'ultimo trillo)* is an intense, refreshing poem. The death of a bird was a scene not unfamiliar to Rebora in his walks through the woods. Here he tells of a little bird that trustingly responds to the decoy only to fall into the trapper's hands. And to the last, the bird remains oblivious of the cruel deception and even greets death with a trill:

> The nets are set in the thicket:
> the little bird at the luring calls
> wings about and alights, lively and loving;
> it flutters in the cunning
> hands a while, then death
> issues from its bill with a last trill.

The bird alighted, thinking it was in answer to a love call. For the poet such a death is but to be envied. The wickedness of the trapper is almost overlooked as we admire the bird's swift, trusting answer to the call. What gives beauty and value to our acts is not the outcome but the love that inspires them. The closing lines express the poet's wish for a similar end: "That is how I would like to fall after my heart;/ how I would end my days: with a generous cry." Rebora was able to avoid a sentimental treatment of the subject by his conciseness and by the novel and joyous interpretation of an otherwise sad end. *"L'ultimo trillo"* is no tragedy. It is a joyful acceptance of the very destruction of life. The bird's ecstatic caroling in so bleak a scene is, for Rebora, a message of hope.

In the poem "The Comforter" *(Il consolatore)* Rebora sees life in all its reality. It is the vision of a profound individual; the vision of a seeker of light in the darkness; the vision of an ardent person who would forget all else and only love. He is a practical, concrete person who wants to be "The Comforter."

Frammenti lirici

> And here, without shelter or escape,
> without deception or flight
> I live in time with desire;
> and my pulse is of the blood of all.
> Like a song in melody,
> like a note in harmony,
> I manifest myself in love of people:
> and my voice seems vile to me
> when it, hardly my own, tormentedly loses its way.
> Like a deep vein at the roots,
> like a fruitful rain,
> I try to be reborn in happy fellow-beings:
> and grimly I thirst when renunciation
> turns me shut where I was open.
> As a mother in time of famine
> gives all the bread to her children,
> even so I like to comfort others
> while I roll inside.

VII   *Search for Truth*

The autobiographical element in the *Frammenti lirici* becomes a continuous song of torment-search-for-Truth. His fragments are lyrical meditations, where Rebora's breathing is his poetry. Mysteriously, he finds himself where the apparent and the invisible, the human and the divine, are entwined and confounded. His desire to know reality, and his suffering due to the tremendous contradictions of life, are reechoed in the poem "My Voice" *(La mia voce):*

> Let every man open up his whirlpool and let it flow
> brooklike into the water of others.
> Anxious pressing questions come
> from the free flight of the celestial sphinxes
> tied to our passing
> that knows faint answers:
> on lands and on seas
> men, restless, seek one another out avariciously
> purging in blood hidden sorrows. . . .

Rebora's voice, full of exultation, hope, eternity, is an inspired voice that seeks to eradicate sorrow and eliminate tears while it wants to console and love mankind. The poem is an acknowledgment of the existence of eternity:

> O eternal voice in transient motion
> revealing the future Calvary
> of beleaguered goodness!
> O Voice, rise again from the heart of every man
> above the mockery and diversity
> of unrelieved anxiety:
> and every man, where he dies, will discover
> who was waiting for him to live.

Rebora had already spoken of his communion not only with things, but with life and with mankind. In *"La mia voce"* he goes beyond. He offers us a true code of human conduct filled with Christian charity. He believes in goodness, in love, in dedication:

> But here is a heart and it would like
> to find other hearts;
> while the instant bleeds
> this voice is irony:
> but here is love and it would like
> to kindle more love;
> while hunger and tragedy
> desire and anxiety
> rapaciously claw
> in the brain and in the senses.
> Come here, you cursed Poetry,
> to see beauty
> to taste goodness:
> but here is help and it would like
> to call for more help.
> Let every man say where he is lost,
> and in the blended voice
> let him find approval and correction.
> Let sorrow soothe like fatigue
> which brings sleep to renew the vigil,
> let sorrow unravel like the day
> that toppling creates the morrow,
> let sorrow live like a good mother
> that draws her hope from suffering,
> let sorrow glow like a lantern
> that from our path unveils to others, theirs.

Frammenti lirici

Rebora has abandoned his solitude. He is now participating in the worldly pleasures he had hitherto disdained, and strives to enlighten us in the poem "Invisible Love" *(L'invisibile amore):*

> Space, porous and thirsty,
> from skies and lands drinks back up,
> instantly and unsatedly,
> and dissipates as it receives
> in the echo buzzing from below
> the twenty-four-hour creature;
> but here everyone in the bustle
> stands aside from the others a lord,
> and in the line of his gaze has the universe;
> all else to him is vain or perverse:
> thus from the shore through the water there
> quivers ventlike a gleam of moonlight
> to the passerby, who sees darkness all around.
> Star caught in nebular glare,
> night sucked out of the heart of sunsets,
> drop indistinct in the roar of the sea,
> cliff submerged in the slope of mountains,
> plant scattered while rooting deeply,
> power hidden from machines and fruitful,
> nameless cart-dragging nag,
> do tell the mysterious manner
> of invisible love
> to us, who, poor wretches,
> stamp with our seals
> the work of God
> crying: I, I, I!

CHAPTER 9

Poesie varie

REBORA'S FIRST VOLUME OF POETRY, *Frammenti lirici,* HAD BEEN dedicated "To the First Ten Years of the Twentieth Century." With vivid immediacy he again used these themes in the *Poesie varie* (1913 - 1918). Stressing the more human aspects of life, he made himself the prophet and apostle of a new humanity founded on peace and brotherhood.

In the short period between the publication of the *Frammenti lirici* and his departure for the battlefields of World War I, Rebora published several other poems. Among them were *"Il ritmo della campagna in città," "Fantasia di carnevale," "Notte a bandoliera,"* and *"Clemente, non fare così!"* With regard to the last poem, Marino Moretti, who published it, wrote to Prezzolini rather uncomplimentarily: "I met Rebora by chance and asked for some poetry. He sent me a *fragment* which . . . never ended. It seemed a little like broth that is 'stretched.' But I published it just the same. . . ."[1] But Moretti was wrong. "Clemente, don't do that!" is one of Rebora's longest and most characteristic poems, and he referred to it in his letters to friends and to his brother Piero:

> You know my keen awareness of reality-truth, apparently abstract, but instead the very substance of all (even of the little pen which blackens this paper); and the overwhelming frenzy of forces and ideas now reborn in you, places us more than ever in the whirlpool of a single river ("I obey/ the god that increases, and the devil adds to:/ dissension, creative everywhere/ ephemeral, eternal, with typical presence;/ Reality, immense fear, flees etc."). Only, what we hypostatize as "bourgeoisie" is not something to exclude in order to achieve salvation (and beautiful teeth of sated hunger): nor is it an obstacle to be removed in order to achieve (augment) something in time and space; all is without beginning or end and all that is hated or loved is perpetual suicide reborn, *noneliminable.* Therefore I feel this life

Poesie Varie

situation thus and so, without a before or after, and above all without a hierarchy of values, and without a goal (fatality-freedom of every mixture, that has nothing outside itself).[2]

These thoughts and verses sent to his brother Piero are also found in another letter, dated February 12, 1912, addressed to Antonio Banfi, as well as in the poem "Clemente, don't do that!"

> O mother, I shouldn't? I obey the
> god that increases and the devil adds to:
> dissension, creative everywhere
> ephemeral, eternal, with typical presence.
> Reality, immense fear, flees,
> and the world as it produces is truth:
> a desperate defense is our world,
> that seems certain again in the end
> dissolves in that
> perpetual transmutation
> perpetual suicide
> without before or after, unitedly,
> and it is no merit, it is no sin,
> if in this matter-laden flow
> everyone, a sleeping, tossing boy,
> turns his anxious spires
> to the meaning of things.

Gently reproaching him, Rebora's mother seeks to help him analyze his behavior:

> Clemente, don't do that
> serene and merciless
> forbid with sadness
> the good nature I gave
> to my dear, saintly you;
> why? . . . .

Rebora realizes he must make a choice and tries to explain his actions:

> But feel me still as your son,
> loved left by pure souls,
> by swift childhood friends;

if I set afire native impulses
or upset pretexts of the game.
But leave me space to suffer:
there are so many years
in the time to come!
And perhaps, tomorrow, in my thirties
(the awful choice is pressing,
to say yes, say no
to something I know),
and perhaps, tomorrow . . . .

I *Childhood*

Rebora returned to his childhood days. He recalled the loving yet severe faces of his family, when he needed their warmth and understanding. In this, too, Rebora was a modern man. Undoubtedly he was filled with emotional and psychological complexes which gave him much anguish. That is why the recollection of his early years—years of happiness—filled him with sentiments of nostalgia. He felt alone and already mysteriously aware that sooner or later he must make the "awful choice" *(la scelta tremenda)* and endeavored to return to his mother to free himself from the responsibility of a fatal decision. In fact, these lines, *"(urge la scelta tremenda, /dire sì, dire no/ a qualcosa ch'io so),"* may be called the key to Rebora's future. The poet describes his life, lived in "populated solitude!" *(popolata solitudine!),* as it swiftly passes on:

> But that does not offend me;
> to live is to justify oneself.
> I alone know
> that in body and in soul
> unmistakable appearance
> this is the way I am today; and for what I shall be
> I do not mortgage my future.

He speaks of the many mischievous tricks, and how he used to tease his little sister Marcellina:

> But many were the days
> that the sum total hurt:
> there had again been tears; and daddy,

Poesie Varie

>arriving for supper, would gaze at me
>and shake me
>as just and perturbed he
>as I was glum and sore,
>in shame often running away
>from my brothers
>I would fast out my spite in bed.
>And you, mama, a little later,
>tucking in the bedcovers,
>bent over, by glances,
>with a kiss would whisper:
>Clemente, don't do that!

While it is true that these *fragments* are somewhat different from his earlier poetry, one must add that their tone and vivacity are so sincere and characteristic that they must be considered in the same category.

II *The Marketplace*

The impressionistic, onomatopoetic *"Il ritmo della campagna in città,"* published in 1913, is a painting in which Rebora was captivated by the life that surrounded him and fell in with the rhythm of rural life transferred to the marketplace in Milan. Notwithstanding the essential unity in Rebora's poetry, this is a rather unique genre poem. In a letter to Prezzolini, Rebora, the lover of the common man, characteristically wrote: "It is a nought [a trifle] of color and life" *(È un niente di colore e vita).*[3]

On a warm, festive August morning, when much of the city was on vacation, Rebora walked toward a fruit and vegetable market in Milan. He was attracted by the luring calls of the fruit vendors. Occasionally their cries were interrupted; but then someone else could be heard singing at the top of his lungs a patriotic refrain which dated back to the Turco-Italian war of 1911: "Tripoli, beautiful land of love" *(Tripoli, bel suol d'amore).*

The poet gives a realistic description of the people who flock to the marketplace. He comments on the dress of the women, on the shouting fruit vendors who cunningly attract and distract buyers:

>The fruit vendors hawk
>expertly peeling baskets

>   from the tiered planks,
>   tidying up their carts
>   that from clever spots
>   ambiguous of price and looks
>   invite to partake those breathing
>   the stench of asphalt
>   on this treeless August
>   in the city that, gaunt and informal,
>   readily retrieves its dialect.

Rebora stops to buy grapes. He takes in one hand the paper cone in which the grapes have been short-weighed, protecting it with the other from the shoving passersby. He holds the cone high, and since it is close to his mouth, he is tempted to taste the fruit. He takes from the vendor his sullied change:

>   . . . and in the tide
>   I turn around, protect,
>   tidy sideways with my lip
>   the grapes hanging
>   from the paper cone.

Suddenly he is aware of the black eyes of an urchin watching him with watering mouth. He gives him a penny, saying: "Here, boy, a penny and beat it!" The boy buys a penny's worth of loose grapes while the poet keeps pecking at his cluster.

Sold by the vendor's shouted praise of his apples and pears, the poet buys three of each, stuffing his pockets and foretasting their sweetness as he strokes the bulging side of his coat. While working his way through the milling crowd, he observes now someone merging with and soon disappearing into the crowd, now someone grumbling at the shoves that nearly knocked off his bundles, now someone busy with figures, hugging his baskets in his lap, or someone going back and again leaving in a huff, the better to strike a bargain; or finally someone who sneakingly looking about, swears, between spittings and removals of pipe,

>   While the tide surges and changes
>   down the naughty street
>   ebbing from the flash of the avenue
>   amid streaks of sunshine

>   with deafening words
>   in mirrored brilliance of devilish tricks.

"Il ritmo della campagna in città" is not only a genre painting portraying a city scene at the marketplace, but a joyous celebration as well. It is a combination of colors, of sounds. The poet forgets himself, his problems, his anguish, his ideals. He merely looks and listens and, in a sense, allows himself to be swept away by this wave of life that envelops him in Milan.

In contrast with other poems of the period which are almost always agitated by the violence of his passions, this work is a welcome change in that it makes the ones that follow more dramatic, as has been noted already in the poem *"Clemente, non fare così!"*

III Poems of Passion

During this period, among other poems, Rebora published *"Movimenti di poesia"* in four parts. He later disowned parts III and IV in the Vallecchi edition of *Le Poesie* (1913 - 1947). These parts are of a sentimental nature, inspired by his association with Lydia Natus.

For all his eagerness to publish these four fragments, Rebora called them *"antipatici e forse poco facili"* in a letter to Boine,[4] adding that he would like to have them published because he felt he was changing *(sento che muto)*. In Part I he reminisces about playing with his niece Enrica, who used to call him "zio Checche," a name Rebora delighted in using when referring to himself. In Part II he writes with tender irony:

>   I drink my weight
>   distracted surprised
>   that life seems certain
>   without hearing look out, look out. . . .
>   And I drift along
>   pushed standing, in chaos
>   toward burning clamors,
>   under skies mixed
>   of glances without pardon.

In Part IV Rebora expresses his love for his Russian friend

Lydia, calling her *"Lucciola"* (firefly) as he describes their moments of intimacy mingled with joy and anguish:

> And you, perverse
> dark firefly
> who tempt me in the shadow
> and you still do not dazzle me,
> smooth alga of light
> sensuously veiled
> who lay the traps
> and ignore my kisses!
> Then suddenly awakened,
> cut at the peak of things,
> I gazed upon the night
> hard on the windowsill,
> in the open carnal shirt:
> in the bitter wave
> the room upside down
> and the furniture dark;
> and shining forth short
> lost in the abyss
> I slid my head into torpor.
>
> But at dawn, on awakening,
> in the sudden tearing away
> how many lamps went out,
> how many grips of hooks pressed me!
> Your allurement,
> your loving sorrow,
> my assent increased
> that you may grip it,
> that it may reveal the inert nature
> to each, the fortune
> in this anxiety of an
> avidly superb ambush.
> I know that my mouth will suck a poison
> of a dangerous sweetness,
> but beautiful and more fervent
> than all health, all certainty:
> of you, your too easy
> solitary strength;
> I know that people clinging
> to the pretext of the world
> will deny my grace
> with hard-toothed lip smiles

Poesie Varie

> will rejoice with a whisper:
> "you too, in the sinuousness of the hour,
> you too, on cunning paths,
> you too, just like the others!"

Apparently Rebora is no longer the same. His life had been independent and free. Now he indulges in sensual pleasures, joining friends in drinking, and adapting himself to a new life-style. As one examines his correspondence the change that has taken place may be fully understood.

Rebora's life had been an exemplary one for his family and friends. When he lived with Lydia Natus in her apartment at Via Tadino, 3, he experienced erotic pleasures for eight days which seemed like eternity. So he explained his new life-style to his brother Piero, saying that they enjoyed each other while drinking beer and in the midst of his heavy teaching schedule; he felt like a giant because he had become acquainted with the poverty of a semi-intelligent and semicorrupt world (poets, literary people, etc.) His words are clear: "I made the passing acquaintance of a woman (an artiste-cocotte, exasperated and underestimated by imbeciles who thus deprive her of her magnificent sulphuric acid); after I heard her, I destroyed almost all I had left of my 'lofty' artistic-philosophical writings, etc., etc., the fruit of *fear,* of avoiding the risk (there you have 'the philosophers', etc.).[5]

To his friend Angelo Monteverdi, Rebora wrote, "Haven't you fashioned for yourself a static (= *stitico* [constipated]) Clemente, and if I were *to change him,* would you be sorry? I say that because for a month now—even though I am still the old devil or virgin god, with power and freedom—implacable against my too *easy* (!?) dry, largely solitary bliss, I have been forcing (or owing) my destiny to new life experiences, the last one of which is perhaps about to ask for all the courage in me, anguished and joyous lawgiver of my all and of my nothing. And this, at the cost of *accepting myself* even in what for others—who conceive human 'fatalities' as spiderwebs already woven—I shall appear fallen, straying, and a thousand similar foolish names."[6]

And to Antonio Banfi shortly after, Rebora spoke of a solitary "bliss," in reference to his life prior to his friendship with Lydia Natus and to his new life-style:

About myself I do not have energy to tell you; I have already written to friends—and acquaintances!—and spoken in person with many I love because of the need to unload a little the exuberance of my implacable fate. I shall tell you only that for months I have been a natural flowing lava, and for twenty-five days, all a nature that will topple any day. I couldn't care less! I cannot clarify this: I have *forced* my destiny into complete love; I was too ashamed of my solitary "bliss," of my model-life (imagine passing for a man who *chose* the "lofty and luminous and intense" life, as they say, putting aside comparisons, to be somewhat like a little Christ or Beethoven or Nietzsche! Instead, I'll upset them all, that is, myself. And war rages everywhere! For me it has always been thus; so what is new?). How difficult it is for me—and delicious—*to enjoy*, to have the "comforts" of a mad passion; I was accustomed to ecstasies quite other than these! But at the same time I bless the woman whom I carry away in my flaming whirlwind—will we go to the dogs?—and if tomorrow a gun bullet should take away this neat vast tension, good-bye, my beautiful one, good-bye!⁷

These last words, *"Addio, mia bella, addio,"* are the opening words of a song popular since the days of the Risorgimento: "Good-bye, my beautiful one, good-bye, / the army is departing,/ if I were not also leaving/ it would be cowardice" *(Addio, mia bella, addio,/ l'armata se ne va,/ se non partissi anch'io/ sarebbe una viltà)*. But here it means no more than "Good-bye and good luck!"

CHAPTER 10

Russian Interlude

REBORA WAS ATTRACTED BY LYDIA NATUS,[1] WHOSE TALENT AS A concert pianist was recognized in Milan. He had met her in 1908 at a concert in the home of the Consul of Holland. She was the wife of a Milanese industrialist, who had been sent to prison for embezzlement soon after their marriage. It was not until 1914, while her husband was in jail, never to be reunited with her, that her acquaintance with Rebora became love.

Not long after, Rebora ceased to see in her an artiste-cocotte, as he had described her to his brother. Instead he saw a bereaved mother (her child had died in infancy) and wife. Then, caught in a magnificent, but terrible, entanglement with this woman of "infinite love," he decided to move in with her and "suffer being adored by her." At the same time he encouraged his friend Boine to continue to be her friend and, should he perish in the war, to be her "protector." It was indeed a "tragic" love affair.[2] They could not marry, there being no procedures for divorce in Italy. Lydia's sensual, artistic temperament was not in keeping with his spiritual dispositions! And the cohabitation was not an unbroken bliss, as she explained to their mutual friend Giovanni Boine:

> Do not think, I beg you, that I enjoy great happiness and nothing else and that my love for Clemente is solely an ecstasy, a continuous sweet beatitude. If you knew everything! If you could only have an inkling of how much sorrow, universal sorrow, there is in our love, in our union. . . . As soon as we fell in love, we became united *without hope*. How tragic our life has been since then . . . and each smile of mine or his, each ray of sunshine, each minute of sweetness I spent with him, oh if you knew how much, and how bitterly, cruelly, I had to and must still pay for, always, always. I cannot have a half day of peace, of light with him without there rising some displeasure, some difficulty, some sorrow. Internal war, external war. And

just think, he is being drafted . . . and I shall remain alone here, without him, in mortal anguish; oh if he, *he* had the superhuman goodness, a strong hand and great courage to kill me how grateful I would be to him! And I *am determined* if he should not return, if God should take away even this my last oasis of serenity, of faith, of hope, of beauty and of life, to follow him, indeed I will, there whence there is no return. At least if I could join him then and die close to him as a firefly dies when the ray of sunshine is too strong: dazzled, it dies of love.[3]

The ménage lasted several years. Only once her husband visited them in their apartment. He was welcomed with "kisses and embraces," as she recalled years later in a letter to the author: "It was a marvelous day full of human pardon. He asked me for my photograph and I offered it to him with a white rose and the small amount of money I could afford, and a good glass of wine. It was one of the most divine hours that I spent with him which made me suffer so much. . . ."[4]

Both she and Rebora survived her husband, who died in 1931, in view of which she thought it incredibly strange that she was the cause of Rebora's future religious state. For, if she had not gone to Paris in 1919, Rebora would not have become a priest, and they would have legalized their union at her husband's death. But then how could they have known that he would die before them?

Two months earlier, speaking of his intense, loving compassion for Lydia, Rebora revealed the nature of this "tragic love" in a letter to Sibilla Aleramo:[5]

As for me, . . . I sling away my days in the onrush of my profession . . . , and in the brief eddies (oh vast!) with the creature that is burning with me. A woman who has found it in her to love a man such as I; and maybe she will face the fatal weight of my tireless gravitating toward the beyond. With her I feel very far away and very close; and the more she unfolds under my warmth, the more I should like to leave her. It is unbelievable how everything becomes episodic for me, and what for other people might constitute an inexhaustible fullness, for me instead is too little as against what I feel. I will be going to Russia with her this coming June, if nothing changes. Meanwhile I am studying a little Russian: and I will be plunging into uncertainty. However, Aleramo, you must feel in my dryness all my tenderness and marrow-deep affection for this woman, in her kind, very great, incomparably rich mother and lover.

Approximately one year after his departure for military

Russian Interlude,

service, Rebora was in the front lines and became afflicted with a nervous trauma. Lydia managed to have him relieved of active duty. She then nursed him back to health, contacted his friends for various publications, encouraged him to write poetry, to compose music. She herself even put one of his poems, *"Stella mia"*[6] to music.

I *Introduction to Russian Letters*

Lydia taught Rebora the Russian language and he became greatly interested in Russian literature, especially that which exalted goodness, simplicity, the poor in spirit, or what described the work, anxiety and misery of ordinary people. He understood deeply the immortal characters created by the genius of Dostoevski and Tolstoi. He was one of the few Italian writers who translated directly from the Russian during this period. His translations[7] ceased when Lydia Natus left him, after seeing him through his battle-caused psychoneurosis.

This Russian interlude was a consequence of the spiritual crisis which had been caused by the war. For Rebora the war was useless slaughter, a horrible massacre, an incomprehensible and bestial display of cruelty. He believed in the dignity of all mankind, in man's inalienable right to respect, understanding, and love. He wanted every man to be given the possibility to live in peace and in beauty. But reality was so different from his dream—and he suffered profoundly as he felt the evils imposed on his brothers, whoever and wherever they might be. He understood the tragedy of man. And he found in the great Russian masterpieces that sense of Christian unity and charity which he unconsciously craved and so much of which, unfortunately, had been either forgotten or condemned.

It is significant that Rebora chose Russian authors like Andreyev, Tolstoi, and Gogol for translation. Still more significant is what he selected: the biblical story of "Lazarus," the story of "the Christians," stories of despair, family, love. Like them, he was bent on improving the moral and social conditions of the period. Like them, he preached the need for soul-searching and simplicity of life.

Rebora does not translate mechanically; he succeeds in reproducing the art and the poetry of Andreyev, Tolstoi, and Gogol; he penetrates their intimate problems; he renders sensations, developments, and foreign expressions with Italian substitutes and, where none exist, he recreates them with genuine freshness of poetic expression.

Rebora's Russian translations may be said to close his "Romantic period." They merit study. The first, *Lazarus and Other Stories (Lazzaro e altre novelle),* by Leonid Andreyev,[8] consisted of six short stories: "Lazarus," "The Christians," "The Marseillaise," "The Stranger," "Phantoms," "Ben Tobit." The stories have explanatory notes and are preceded by a foreword.

Piero Gobetti, founder of *La rivoluzione liberale,* called Rebora's work "a translation of highest artistic value," and classified it "a masterpiece."[9] Even the most insignificant passages, episodes, and nuances are rendered with delicate and impeccable faithfulness. In order to show his intimate, harmonious translation, Gobetti compares Rebora's translation of "The Christians" with one found in the *Biblioteca universale.* While this Sonzogno edition gives us the purely literal meaning, Rebora succeeds in maintaining the sense of the supernatural and of wonderment, which corresponds with Andreyev's meaning. In the translation, one still reads Andreyev, whose lines have not been betrayed by Rebora: *"Dietro le finestre cadeva novembrina neve dimoiata, ma nell'edificio del tribunale c'era invece tepore, animazione e buonumore tra quelli . . ."* (Outside the windows November sleet was falling, but in the courthouse there was, instead, tepidness, liveliness and good humor among those . . .).

Rebora presents all the characters in these short stories with Andreyev's refinement and delicacy: the incomprehensible nostalgia of "The Stranger," the fearful isolation of the souls in "The Christians," the horrible encounter of life and death in "Lazarus," the description of life among the insane in "Phantoms." These characters belong to Andreyev's artistic world which does not distinguish truth from illusion, where art and thought form a single palpitating reality, and the complex spiritual problems of the past are the drama of the present. This is Rebora's world.

In a review of *Lazzaro e altre novelle,* Francesco Meriano[10] acknowledges Rebora as "obviously playing an important part in the interpretation of this Russian masterpiece, which he has dressed with his conceptual phraseology, his harmonious rhythm.

Russian Interlude

Rebora is a poet of rare and not ephemeral qualities, who has had moments of true greatness, who rarely writes, achieving with difficulty the possibility of expressing the world that whirls through his spirit. No one was more suitable than he to render in Italian Andreyev's short stories."[11]

In his short stories Andreyev probed individuals in the traditional style of Russian Realism. With this translation, Rebora gave the Italian reader an opportunity to appreciate Andreyev who, using the allegory and symbol, was a seeker after the hidden motives of human actions.

Rebora was pleased with Meriano's favorable review. Writing to express his appreciation, he added that he had just completed the translation of *La felicità domestica* by Leo Tolstoi[12]—its title in the English version is *Family Happiness*—stating that he had worked for six months, and had put love and music into it.[13]

Meriano had planned a series of special issues for his review, *La Brigata*, and asked Rebora to prepare the first one on Russia, to acquaint the Italian public with the best of contemporary Russian poets, writers, painters, and musicians. (A French issue by Guillaume Apollinaire would follow.) Unfortunately the revolutionary events that took place interfered and only the first page of Igor Stravinsky's unpublished manuscript excerpt from *Les Noces (Villageoises)*,[14] which the composer had given to Rebora in 1917, appeared in *La Brigata*, with an expression of the hope of publishing the special issue at some future time since "these precious Russian friends" could no longer collaborate at this time.

On July 24, 1919, Rebora informed Prezzolini that *La felicità domestica* was completed and told him that his translation was the result of "a spiritual prompting and because of my affinity or attraction for the work." He further added that perhaps he would soon lose the precious help of Lydia who, throughout all this work, was his guide and inspiration. He noted too that his intuition made him penetrate into the Russian language as though to issue again from the womb of a mother, hence without "knowing yet how to talk." He concluded by saying he would translate *The Cossacks* or some other "minor" work by Leo Tolstoi or something by Dostoevski,[15] for example, *Nuccia or Annuccia Nisvànoia*, which would oblige him to renew his expressive interpretation *(interpretazione espressiva)*.[16]

Rebora's interest in *The Cossacks* is no surprise. He was aware of the intimate feelings of his readers. If his translations were to have a universal appeal in Italy, he had to select writings which concentrated on the inner life of the individual. The issues had to be moral and psychological. As in his poetry, his mission was to teach, to bring about a moral and social regeneration in order to satisfy his thirst for a moral justification of life.

Perhaps Rebora selected *La felicità domestica* because it is one of the most poetic of Tolstoi's works. Or, perhaps, because it is a magnificent study of a woman's soul and hence an appropriate tribute to the departing Lydia Natus.

The work is the autobiography of a young, passionate, and sensitive woman, who, thrown into the company of her guardian, marries him. She discovers too late that the love which she has to bestow is met by a philosophic liking so cold as to thoroughly disenchant her. Though she drifts toward the chasm of illicit passion, she manages to retain a certain serenity and happiness returns through her acceptance of the inevitable and in her devotion to duty.

In reading the work, one comes to identify with this young woman and feel as she did—her love, her sorrow, her happiness. And everywhere there is music and poetry and beauty. The poetic passages filled with fascinating descriptions of country life brought back memories to Rebora. No doubt his own sentiments are reflected throughout the work. Perhaps it reflects what had happened to him and Lydia during their period together.

When Rebora finished this translation, he wrote to his mother that he would be lying if he denied that he was proud of the work he had done.[17]

La felicità domestica vividly describes the inner conflicts of its protagonist as she passed through a period of intense self-searching. In the foreword Rebora writes: ". . . This image of love that one seeks . . . has reverberations of present experiences. . . . The sentiments, the places, the persons—all were truth for the writer, and is reality for us." Thus Rebora's own search for truth continued until his conversion, when he embraced the doctrine of Christian love wholeheartedly, and dedicated himself to the propagation of brotherly love as a member of the Rosmini Fathers.

Again in translating Nikolai Gogol's *The Overcoat (Il Cappotto)*[18] Rebora was prompted by his desire to propagate universal brotherhood, love for the humble, compassion for the suffering. It is a realistic tale dealing with the humble and downtrodden of St. Petersburg, Russia. It was unusual in Gogol's time to have a common man as the protagonist of a book. But Rebora, whose sympathies were for those who were suffering, comments on the need for renunciation, sacrifice, duty: ". . . every sacrifice, worthy of the name, is an incomparable good; and it is marked by a breath of freedom that increases in us when we make it spontaneously." In conclusion, he writes: "When one lives with such consistency, with devoted trust, then, sooner or later, what one is inside one is also outside, and one's life starts to be a testimonial or rather it reaches an indiminishable accomplishment; in fact an idea can be refuted, but the reality of an example is irrefutable."

On September 14, 1922, Rebora thanked his friend Sibilla Aleramo for her letter regarding *The Overcoat,* in which she commented:

> The pages you wrote using as a pretext Gogol's story contain so much of your thought and faith that one must take them in for their own sake and let them work in us, as a message and a revelation, vouchsafing the good Gogol but one distant smile. Dear Clemente, how many things I relived in reading you! Since that first summer evening when I heard you speak—eight years ago? —and you already had your translucid imagination of a spiritual world, your feverish desire of a full harmony completely inward, feverish because there pulsated in you (as in me, as in all), terrible and marvelous life, the life that is translated into sound into color into figure, into avidity and fatigue, into war, death, remembrance.

In answer to her letter, Rebora said that by recognizing some goodness in him toward her, she was also recognizing it in herself, and it was for that very goodness he was always and confidently knocking at her soul. "I am trying and shall try to be deserving of my mission to unite hearts," he added, "showing them the action of Life, in the very small circle of my possibility; and I thank you for believing me; and it gives me strength to do better."[19] It is interesting to note that, besides *The Overcoat,* Rebora translated Gogol's patriotic poem *"Italia."*[20]

II *Lydia Natus*

Rebora often referred to Lydia by the endearing name

"Lidusa," not only in his letters, but also in the dedication of his books: *"A Lidusa, mia iniziatrice"* (To Lidusa, my initiatrix) in *Lazzaro e altre novelle;* *"A Lidusa, lucciola della luce"* (To Lidusa, firefly of light), in *La felicità domestica.*

Another name by which Rebora called Lydia during this Russian interlude was *"Lucciola."* Among the lyrics he transcribed into an album[21] for her, may be found "The Well and the Firefly" *(Il pozzo e la lucciola)* and "Firefly, I enclosed you" *(Lucciola, io ti chiudevo).* The name *"Lucciola"* was used in both prose and poetry, for example, *"Movimenti di poesia."*

These love lyrics undoubtedly reveal a novel and very interesting aspect of Rebora's life, both human and poetic. They represent freshness and spontaneity, as well as sensitivity, and often portray limpid, original, exquisite images, for example, *"chiocciolina all'ascella dei rami"* (pretty snail in the armpit of branches), and *"farfallina sulla guancia dei frutti"* (pretty butterfly on fruit cheeks). There are also virile, strong images: *"ciuffi d'altezza per l'onda dei monti"* (tufts of height along the billowing mountains), and *"solitudine alata in ghirlanda"* (solitude wing-spread garlandlike). Love makes the usual harshness and crudity in Rebora's poetry disappear, and diminishes its intensity, as in *"Lucciola, io ti chiudevo":*

> Firefly, I locked you up
> in my hand as in my heart,
> so that in the tenuous shadow
> the throbbing lamplight
> might look to you like a huge sun.
>
> Firefly, I did not realize
> that your life is elsewhere,
> on airy hopes
> a welling up of lights
> as many as the stars.
>
> Firefly, I open my hand:
> let me be left with the mad
> phosphorus in my veins,
> and you with the warm gleam
> of a sheltering cradle.

Rebora's love for Lydia Natus cannot be ignored. It is clear that his life changed after his conversion to Catholicism; and if he loved this woman, even beyond the moral and material help they exchanged, if he loved her in the full sense of the word, it did not detract from his future sanctity. The greater the obstacles and the more complicated the ties that bound him to the earth, the stronger and more merciful was the Grace that freed him.

CHAPTER 11

The Ordeal of War

IN THE YEARS PRECEDING WORLD WAR I, THE TRIPLE ALLIANCE among Austria-Hungary, Germany, and Italy had been weakened by Italy's agreements with Great Britain and a rapprochement with neighboring France. Italians had become aware of the change in the European balance of power. Many clamored for the annexation of Austro-Hungarian border districts inhabited by Italians: the Trentino, the city of Trieste, and the areas nearby. And on May 23, 1915, less than a year after Italy had decided on nonintervention, an ultimatum was sent to Austria-Hungary. Hostilities began the following day.

The Italian experience in the Turco-Italian war of 1911, and the Balkan wars of 1912 and 1913, led Italians to believe that the war would last just a few weeks. Italian patriots favoring the war did not foresee the suffering, the disruption of the economy, and the tension that the war would cause. They never envisioned the defeat of Caporetto, the loss of entire army corps, or the enemy occupation of eastern Venetia. Only the American intervention brought hope. The Italian offensive in October of 1918 progressed, and hostilities ended on the Italian front with the armistice of Villa Giusti on November 4. With the signing of the armistice between Germany and the Allies on November 11, 1918, World War I came to an end.

I *World War I*

In 1915, World War I brought Rebora to the trenches as a noncommissioned officer at first, soon promoted to second lieutenant. The victim of shell shock, he ended up in a hospital with a psychoneurotic disorder that plagued him for a long time. Having experienced the hatred and cruelties of war, he was all the more impelled to abhor violence in every form, and induced to dream of a bond of brotherhood among all men. These are the sentiments which are found in the prose and verse he contributed to various periodicals in the years 1916 - 1918: *La Raccolta* and *La Brigata* of Bologna, *La Tempra* of Pistoia, *La Lettura* of Milan, *La Diana* of Naples, *Riviera Ligure* of Oneglia. In these writings Rebora's style is rapid, spontaneous, often in dialogue form, with brief, dry statements similar to those of Jahier and others of the group of *La Voce*. They too belong to the literary panorama of this period, to the *"frammentismo"* of *La Voce*.

One can truly say that in Rebora's prose, as in his poetry, new words spurt like sparks from old expressions, or old splendor is reflected in new expressions. There are, to be sure, less careful pages with little artistic value but as an accompaniment to his poetry they too are precious and rich with surprises. While he was not a Futurist, it is no overstatement to say that, with his prose, Rebora helped (if only in a minor way) the movement to free the Italian language from the old disciplined and often archaic and inflated forms of the traditionalists.

Rebora's literary career was an ever-renewing quest, as personal as any confession could be. Yet it transcends the merely personal. His essential biography is directly relevant to his work and to his involvement with one of the most crucial experiences of modern history—World War I.

At the time that Rebora was called to active duty, his friend Giovanni Boine, because of illness, was rejected. As long as his health held up, Boine worked for the Red Cross, bringing supplies to troops behind the lines. In 1914 he made an important contribution toward the morale of the fighting men with his book *Discorsi Militari*. Upon receipt of a copy, Rebora wrote Boine that he had lived what was written when he first served two years of regular service and during the following two years when he was recalled. But that was all far removed from his mind then. Rebora, back in uniform, was reliving his friend's book. When another friend, Alfredo Panzini, visited him, the occasion was recorded in Panzini's *Diario Sentimentale*.[1]

II *Human Relationships*

Only later as a sergeant in the infantry on Mount Podgora in northern Italy did Rebora come to realize the cruel, heartless, futile butchery of war. His tragic experience began in March 1915 when, stationed in a Milan armory with duties to instruct the soldiers, he lectured on the Italian Risorgimento with "military prudence." Revealing his love for humanity, he commented in a letter to Sibilla Aleramo[2] that there was "much humanity, everywhere!" and that in Italy there was only talk, and no action. And to Prezzolini[3] expressing his distaste for rhetorical patriots, he made the same complaint regarding Italy's inactivity, congratulating himself for doing instead of talking, that is, preparing his men for action. Two weeks later he bemoaned to his mother[4] the lack of preparation among the officers, believing that he could only harbor hope for the spirited initiative of the rank and file, whose generosity was greater than that commonly seen in well-to-do persons. In correspondence with his mother he also expressed dissatisfaction with the monotony of army life. Were it not for the marches and the mountains "life would be intolerable among the buckpassing, muddle-headed misfits of the 'official' world: imagine a 'bureacracized' anarchy. Sometimes, those *good* boys, my soldiers, let me hope again and breathe a little. . . . It had to be my luck to have to endure too this unwarlike war, as well as the unintelligent intelligence of the 'cultured' world on free days."[5]

In the midst of uncertainty and spiritual chaos Rebora continued to be interested in *La Voce*. While in Gorlago he met General Siotto-Pintor of the Reserves, a very young-minded and cultured man who had followed with enthusiasm the ideas of modern movements, particularly that of *La Voce*. Not only did he show his liking for Rebora, but he also invited him to visit his home during the summer.[6]

Besides the lovely countryside and the groups of boys and girls who crowded around him wherever he went, Rebora enjoyed the company of his good soldiers, who were very dear to him. He treated them fraternally, consoling those who were lonely. When one of them committed suicide, he sadly tried to understand his action. He was tormented by feelings of guilt when he accepted the services of an orderly—a meek person who "adored" him and whom he used "as little as possible."[7]

Rebora would not appreciate the rhetorical patriots who were aping D'Annunzio. He had understood Italy's sad state of

The Ordeal of War

affairs. In a conversation with Panzini Sergeant Rebora stated: "War must be something enormously serious since people die in it. Otherwise it is immense suffering for the masses, polarized in the will power of a few people who are outside the war. The young dream of the classic war, heroic! It is an anonymous war, German, without even the *beau geste.*"[8]

III The Horrors of War

From Loveno he had written to Sibilla Aleramo: "The war? But from the beginning of life it is—the immense fear without ideas of 'magnificent' existence—and man is aware of it only when it is tangible." Here one seems to find a hint to the reason for his liasion with Lydia—the war which had just started and was sure to involve Italy: "It [war] has become familiar and not for nothing I violated myself in *love* when around the smell of powder was most pungent."[9] His letter to Daria is also revealing for he considers war a horrible, cowardly necessity: "If I am drafted, 'without enthusiasm' I will be all there, with *my* enthusiasm that sees naked and loves its own adversity."[10] And to his dear friend Michele Cascella: "There is still talk of war: and if I go . . . I too will act as if I believed . . . I would be fighting for our country . . . for civilization . . . fighting in fine against all that enhances life by means of death."[11]

Not far from Mount Podgora, Rebora's next destination was the "Carso" on the "Isonzo" section of the battlefield where, notwithstanding the twenty centimeters of mud that surrounded him in "monstrous" autumn, he wrote his father that he was in a safe zone, but within earshot of the enormous death rattle of cannon, which loudly proclaimed "a hymn to brutality," and close to the "real front (the most devilish one) —'invented' thus by newspapers and by . . . the members of the Chamber of Deputies."[12]

While cannon were rolling at the front, Rebora found time to write his mother, asking her forgiveness for not writing sooner and thanking her for the package of goodies and clothing which he shared with his surviving men. "The horror of what surrounds me (what stench from our unburied dead, while *our* own artillery kills us by mistake!). . . . Whoever is in normal life, or at fronts, (or rear fronts!), more 'picturesque,' cannot

imagine what this *routine,* macabre and vain, is like! . . ."[13]
He had to interrupt his letter because of an enemy attack.

His mother was doing Red Cross work in hospitals, working uninterruptedly in the wake of death at the famous Galleria in Milan, going from one window to the next, from one bed to the next. Rebora tried to comfort her through his letters, assuring her of his good health and talking about *duty* and *trust* that he will survive "for what refuses to die in me." . . . "I'll not speak of myself: it is a blessing for your own tranquillity and comfort (even in case—far be it from me! —of a mishap) that you are not aware of the moral mire, the pity and horror of what is going on here; that you know of events only from the daily rags that deceived and are deceiving the country, and all you mothers!"[14]

On December 3, 1915, Rebora told Lavinia Mazzucchetti that the voice of his friends reaching him sounded strange to him

like an invitation to a dance to a man with a noose around his neck. . . . I am here—after a period of slaughter on [Mount] Podgora—resting (?) in mud up to my eyes, commander of a Company (rather of a cave-dwelling herd), being its only surviving officer. How fortunate you all are to have only "psychological" pains —and you can in no way even imagine. One hundred thousand [Edgar Allan] Poes, but with a mentality between that of a butcher and *routinier,* condensed the two into one simple expression, could give a vague idea of the state of mind here. One lives and dies just as one would spit: corpses lying unburied, like an unprocessed paper—the whole thing in collapsed military exasperation. I no longer know how to write or express myself: I'll know—not that I wish to—when I shall sing, for I do not intend to die.[15]

The perpetual slaughter became a trivial, monotonous practice. Rebora thought of himself as an anonymous Count Ugolino of Dante's *Inferno* in the midst of the stench of living and dead bodies. He wished that the gentlemen who had remained very comfortable "city warriors would have their turn on the battlefield." To his mother, he wrote that his nerves were shot from overfatigue after many months of work and Clementine sacrifice. He added that "after having been nominated for a medal of honor, etc — I've been severely punished on account of someone else's fault, on account of my having been too much a Christ and a poet! . . . My men's affection serves to keep the poison from reaching my heart. —And then there is a creature [he refers to Lydia Natus] who is working to save my light. And I want to return strong—and embrace you all."[16]

IV Shell Shock

Gradually losing his strength, he saw the need for rest, and did not wish to die before accomplishing his mission. He hoped that a furlough would not be jeopardized by harm inflicted by the enemy or by his responsibilities as the commanding officer. But his expectations were dashed. As a consequence of a shock received from the explosion of a heavy cannon and the nervous breakdown caused by the stress and strain of months spent in front-line trenches, he was hospitalized, first in the rear lines and then in Milan.

After recovering from the shock, he was given a long furlough, never to return to the fighting lines. Several years before his death, in one of his notebooks Rebora himself diagnosed his condition as "Mania of the eternal."[17] He described the moments of crises on his way to a psychiatric hospital in Reggio Emilia, and later at Mombello, where he used to accompany the director, a friend of his, on his visits to other patients. He related how, through these experiences, he was later able to help and comfort people who had psychiatric problems. In fact, one evening he endangered his own life, trying to control a youth in a Milan hotel who was fanatically pointing a gun. But he could not disarm him. Finally his screams aroused the staff and they were both thrown out of the hotel.

Rebora had another friend among his superior officers at the front: Captain Giuseppe Martorano, who deeply admired his "good will" and was aware of the noble work he was doing among the soldiers. Unfortunately he was transferred at the time Rebora needed him most. In a letter to the author the captain stated that he immediately recognized in Rebora both intellectual and spiritual superiority—a kind of mystic who endeared himself to all. According to Martorano "Rebora did not understand the war because he felt it was something concocted by wicked people, not an unavoidable historical phenomenon to which one must unavoidably submit."[18] Indeed Rebora felt that war made people deaf to every voice of justice, opaque to every consoling light, arid before so many evils that could be overcome by a simple gesture of loving fraternity. Even on the battlefield he rejoiced in those acts (which fortunately were not missing) that revealed an interior richness, a sense of abnegation, magnanimity, a generous heart. When he heard the sad news about the decimation of the company he had commanded, he wrote to Martorano: "The terrible news you give me was like a hatchet to my heart: I have been mute all day thinking about my Benvenuto, and Soresina and Maioli—and Tagliabue!"[19]

V Scritti di Guerra *in Prose*

Rebora could not believe that all his friends were killed. Heartbroken, he resolved that if he were to survive, he would write and exalt their deaths. This he achieved in the *Scritti di Guerra*. Apparently these writings were to be compiled and published in book form, as Rebora noted in his letter of March 1, 1917, to Francesco Meriano, the editor of *La Brigata:* "I am sending you *'Perdono?'* should you want to use it; it is taken out of my book. I believe I spoke to you about it." In another letter of May 13, 1917, from Villa Serafina (San Colombano al Lambro) in the country where he had gone to recuperate, Rebora explained that because of fatigue he felt that work on the book would nail him to things from which he was struggling to liberate himself—since he did not have sufficient "artistic indifference" to work on it without apprehension. He called it *"un circolo vizioso"* (a vicious circle). But he did not give up. He remained in solitude in the country tilling the land and on May 26, 1917, he wrote again: "My book is progressing—but it hangs over me like a terrible responsibility. I am doing my best in hand-to-hand fighting *(a ferri corti)* with myself so as not to betray anyone." And he told Angelo Monteverdi (June 6, 1917) that he felt obliged to write, whenever possible, what the *"tracollo dell'ora"* (lapsing of the hour) dictated to him: something that few, even among his friends, would recognize.

The book never appeared, but parts of it appeared in magazines in Milan, Bologna, Oneglia, and Naples. In the story *"Dio ci lasciò vedere l'Italia,"*[20] Rebora pretends to gather information from a Russian soldier and describes a horrible situation in which five hundred Italians in a concentration camp are sent to Brennerbach where, upon refusing to dig trenches, they are ordered to prepare themselves for execution. *"Il territoriale consigliato"*[21] is an analysis of Rebora's state of mind

The Ordeal of War

as he observes a soldier on a train and, filled with biting irony, he speaks about the lack of fraternal love among men.

Two of his writings are about his nieces—*"Pensateci ancora"* and *"Bizzarria e corale di retrovia."*[22] In the first, he describes Enrica as she sadly admonishes her elders to "think about the soldiers." The other is centered around her sister Ina, who sends her uncle a drawing of a Prussian soldier.

Rebora's anguish turns to bitterness and rebellion in *"Calendario"* and *"Scampanio con gli angioli."*[23] He portrays the soldiers as a crowd that goes staggering toward a blind destiny in *"Senza fanfara."*[24] In *"Stralcio"* and *"Perdono?"*[25] he inveighs against the war and gives a description of the battlefield which makes one shudder.

There's a vivid scene at the station— *"In orario perfetto"*[26] —where mothers see their sons leave for the trenches and fill the air with their lamentations. The poetic prose passages of *"Coro a bocca chiusa,"* which appeared at the same time, contain all the paroxysm of a disconcerted and disillusioned man as he reviews the tragedy of war.

In his *"Arche di Noè sul sangue,"*[27] Rebora addresses the readers of *La Brigata* and refers to what is happening in the world. He seems to have a presentiment of the revolutions that were about to take place in Russia in 1917, "the 'mondo intellettuale' notwithstanding which feels that the war by now has been liquidated. . . ." The last of the *Scritti di Guerra* is *"Fonte nella macerie,"*[28] which, written in 1915, was published three years later.

As one might expect, there is an intimate connection between the biographical element and his artistic creation: thus his prose faithfully reflects the sentiments which he expressed in letters to his friends. All his writings during this period are the result of his fear and disgust of war, the dissatisfaction he felt, the vague and disturbing desire to fulfill his mission. Through his work, the poet expresses himself passionately. After what he had seen and suffered, all attempts, both literary and political, to idealize and moralize the war could only nauseate him. It was a useless slaughter, a horrible massacre, an incomprehensible and bestial outlet of cruelty. His belief in the dignity of man, in man's ability to live in peace, in his inalienable right to respect, understanding, and love were destroyed. Rebora's dreams as he had presented them in his early poetry were all shattered!

VI *Poetic* Scritti di Guerra

Asked to write of his war experiences,[29] Rebora's answer was that he did not feel up to it. He recalled only "the humble and tragic acceptance of the irreparable," by his men and the "intrepid good sense of the corporals," responsible for whatever little good his company accomplished, commanded as it was by a "stupid or unconscionable" captain whose absurd command caused the death of a sergeant obeying it, "the most modest, luminous and gentle soul, . . . I met with in my company on the Podgora."

Mount Podgora had been the scene of one of the fiercest and bloodiest battles of the entire war. The situation on the front lines was indescribable. Rebora, haunted by the despair of his comrades, found expression in "Viaticum"[30] *(Viatico):*

> O wounded soldier down there in the gully,
> you cried so long for help
> that three hale comrades
> fell for you who almost were no longer.
> Legless trunk
> amid mire and blood
> and your moaning besides,
> have pity on us left
> to gasp for breath and time is endless,
> hasten your agony,
> you can pass away,
> and let that be a comfort to you
> in your insanity incapable of going mad,
> while the slumber on your brain
> holds up the moment,
> leave us quietly—
> thanks, brother.

The poem testifies to Rebora's anguish for suffering humanity. In it one senses the acute awareness of his soldiers' agony and, though an integral part of suffering humanity, he tries to comfort them with the hope they will quietly pass away.

In "Time,"[31] *(Tempo)* Rebora is intensely aware of impending death on the battlefield. He interprets the military predicament as the burden of countless men whose anonymity is acknowledged in his own. Throughout, he speaks of the evanescence of life.

The Ordeal of War

> I open windows and doors,
> but nothing leaves
> no one enters:
> inert inside,
> the air is rain outside—
> drops all fall from a taut thread
> at one jerk.
>
> I open my soul and eyes,
> but no glance leaves
> no thought enters:
> inert inside,
> life is death outside—
> Tears all fall from a taut nerve
> at one jerk.
>
> That which was, is no longer,
> that which will come, will pass away,
> but the present leaves not, enters not
> always taut—
> drops, tears
> at one jerk of time.

Suffering in the trenches and immersed in tragic loneliness, the poet's themes are universal. They are encounters with nature, grief, death, faith, love, hope; encounters with familiar things, with brotherhood, with the mystery of the imponderable world of the spirit.

"Viaticum" and "Time" were published in the magazine *Raccolta*. Later, appearing in the same publication were "The Toad's Serenade" *(Serenata del rospo)*[32] and a charming "Ditty" *(Canzoncina).*[33]

In "The Toad's Serenade," the psychological situation has changed and peace gradually returns to Rebora. Though the nightingale cannot avoid the toad and is swallowed by it, the cheerful bird obligingly continues its tune:

> Parched noonday storm—
> from the topmost branch
> a nightingale in a flash
> has dropped into the thicket:
> the useful toad, there,
> opens wide its sac.

Tunefully sobbing,
now jumping and now flying
it moves on to avoid it—
it blunders into its throat:
the toad, swallows;
later, when nostalgic
peace attunes
night and dawn,
from its sac complaisantly emerges
a mandola tone.

VII *Lydia's Friendship*

During these years Rebora enjoyed Lydia's friendship. Writing to friends he referred to her as his "revelation," his "animator and liberator." She was a "creature" fighting desperately to save him and surround him with tender loving care. Here, in "Ditty," the poet expresses his sentiments with an intensity and freshness that captivate the reader:

If you look at me—
then why don't you kiss me?
and if you kiss me—
then why don't you hug me?

So, if I am sad,
so, if I am happy,
if today is too soon
why, afterwards it will be too late.

But try to call me—
I'll flee away from you:
but try to leave me—
I shall stay with you.

So, if I am sad,
so, if I am happy,
if today is too soon
tomorrow it will be too late.

Tomorrow when it is time
to make love to lady death—
if you but leave me

I will flee from her:
only if you call me,
alas will I stay.

CHAPTER 12

Canti anonimi

REBORA'S SECOND VOLUME OF POETRY, *Canti anonimi,* IS IN A sense a continuation of the *Frammenti lirici,* which constituted the first part of his drama, the human one, that of the follower of Mazzini, of the moralist. The second part is the divine, for Rebora became firmly established in his vocation as a poet and, after having been undenominationally "religious," became a Catholic.

All Rebora's world (his lyrics, his lectures, his translations) encompass his actions, his drama, his developments. His poetry may not be considered *"poesia pura"* because it has been enriched by the fervor of his apostolate, by propaganda, by social content. His poetry is more *preached* than *represented*. It is conceptual, metaphysical poetry.

The *Canti anonimi* was published in 1922. It is introduced by three lines from the poem "Clemente, don't do that!" *(Clemente, non fare così!):* "The awful choice is pressing:/ to say yes, to say no/ to something I know."

Rebora himself declared that his "lyrics belong to a spiritual condition which kept imprisoned in the individual that hope now freeing itself, in certainty of effective goodness, towards an action of faith in the world." His poetry risks being judged as a mission. More than an encounter it may be a dispute, a clash between formal elements (lyrical-artistic) and spiritual elements (ethical propositions, etc.).

In the first poem Rebora begins with a play on the words *ardere* and *ardire: "Non ardito perchè ardente"* (Not daring because ardent). He speaks of fortune being consumed by people, and clearly defines his mission:

> But I gather and keep in my heart

Canti anonimi

>on the deserted road
>all that has been lost:
>then I give some back to whoever has sought.

I *Ringing of Bells*

Rebora's self-abandonment to nature becomes contemplation. He meditates on his immediate surroundings—the city, the streets, the ringing of the bells. One can feel the vivid and tender *"din-don"*—the tolling of the Lombardy bell. It must be recalled, however, that this *"din-don"* is not new in Italian poetry of the twentieth century. But Rebora's bells are different. They are religious bells. There had been Pascoli's bells which were *"tinnule e blande"* (tinkling and soft); Corrado Govoni's silvery bells *"delle povere suore cappuccine"* (of the poor Capuchin nuns); Aldo Palazzeschi's distant and close-by bells of the *"ore sole come solo pane:"* (lonely hours like bread alone). Nor do Rebora's bells remind us of Edgar Allan Poe's bells, for they are neither merry nor rhythmical.

Rebora's "Lombardy Bell" *(Campana di Lombardia)* belongs to a group of *"poesie cantabili"*—one can almost hear the music and song. It is a restful moment—nondramatic in its invitation to nature, to life. It is a sequence of simple lines that reecho ancient folk refrains: "voice, voice fading away/ but causing no sadness" *(Voce, voce che vai via/ e non dai malinconia)*. They are festive rhymes that have the power to cure, to persuade, to find a solution to the *"intimo pianto"*—lines that are beautiful and consoling and profoundly religious. They are fifteen lines *(ottonari,* that is, eight syllables) of which nine rhyme with *melodia.*

>Lombardy bell,
>your voice, my voice,
>voice voice fading away
>but causing no sadness.
>I do not know what it is,
>if whether you are hushed or tolling
>skyward trust rises in me.
>that my inner tears will be stilled,
>if in my bosom is a melody
>asking questions and giving answers,

> if in a cluster of harmony
> sparklingly is transfused
> heart into heart, voice into voice—
> voice voice fading away
> but causing no sadness.

II *Aphorisms*

Rebora's mysticism reaches great heights as he gets closer to his encounter with Christ. In "Sandbags for the Eyes" *(Sacchi a terra),* Rebora gives human qualities to inanimate things; he enjoys playing with words to express his contrasting sentiments; he uses rare words in unusual ways:

> Sandbags for the eyes,
> deep trenches of the hearts—
> the cave-dwelling age is in us.
>
> The home is a meeting place
> by virtue of the soup—
> and when there is none it is a row.
>
> Every affection is a discomfort:
> man a plagiarism
> woman a contagion.
>
> Even the one who loves you is a burden
> if to feel in a twosome
> she makes a pillow of your hours.

In this collection of aphorisms, Rebora is critical of his own commitment and finds it difficult to justify his actions: "Whatever you may say or do/ there is a cry inside:/ that is not why, that is not why! / And thus everything refers back/ to a secret question:/ the act is a pretext." He concludes that each action of his merely serves to avoid questioning himself seriously and continues his self-analysis: "Almost like a mirroring crystal/ merciless is conscience/ to him who gropes opaquely./ On his face there is a furrow/ down which tears flow:/ but his eye withers if he looks."

However, Rebora realizes that no one is truly courageous:

There is a wedge in the heart,
but we dare not remove it
lest the blood gush out.

Work has an ornate handle
and a fast blade
to force open your day.

Hunger swallows wheat—
but then it is straw burning
in a thimbleful of air.

Desire devours the moment:
but within it causes engorgement,
constipation is deep within.

Solitude is life—
but a noose
hangs you on others.

You can, yes, erect high walls
and a convent within yourself:
but the impure soul feeds
on the world it holds in contempt.

It would be a myth were one to think there can be action without the torment of criticism. Indeed, understanding demands increased suffering:

You say: lucky water
that does not fear falling,
and flees at will
following the slope.

Thus would you like to banish the hours
they weary of you,
and time to resolve
what came undone in you

But birds are so light
to give weight to their flight,
and minds too weary
to rise from the ground.

And yet something understood

does not redeem something suffered;
and a kissless word
leaves the lips more lonely.

The poet admonishes those who wish to listen to his maxims. All life develops in ignorance, he explains. It is impossible to achieve one's desires: "An awesome admonition echoes/ but its voice is not present;/ a cradle is heard to whimper/ but the mother is absent./ Flight from a void close by/ toward a void far away,/ the turmoil is a deception;/ it is all a being too late."

Rebora, concerned, continues an examination of conscience:

> The heart which in man
> if it goes down is a bomb
> explodes against a hard obstacle
> and makes a tomb of the present.
>
> If you do not hoist bannerlike your heart,
> rig for yourself the tricolor,
> if you do not reveal humanly the day
> you feign a peace which wages war against the world.
>
> The day today is alone,
> it has its voice in mid-throat;
> its adverse hands,
> one yesterday, the other tomorrow,
> attempt to loosen your knot,
> O freedom, you who cast a lasso
> for an embrace.
>
> But if you offer resistance
> life leaves you behind,
> if you do not squander
> life will not pass you by.
>
> In the imminence of God
> life filches
> ephemeral reserves,
> while everyone clings
> to some treasure of his which shouts to him: good-bye!

Canti anonimi

III "Tense-faced"

From a lyrical viewpoint, perhaps the most beautiful poem of these *Canti* is "Tense-faced" *(Dall'Imagine tesa):*

> Tense-faced
> I keep a watchful eye upon each instant
> with imminence of expectancy—
> yet I expect no one:
> in the lighted shadow
> I peer at the doorbell
> that scatters an imperceptible
> pollen of sound—
> yet I expect no one:
> within four walls
> more space-stunned
> than a desert
> I expect no one.
> But come it must,
> come it will, if I hold out,
> to bloom unseen;
> it will come of a sudden
> when I am least aware;
> it will come as forgiveness
> of all that brings on death;
> it will come to make me certain
> of his treasure and mine;
> it will come as balm
> for my sorrows and his;
> it will come, perhaps already is coming
> his whispered word.

The strength of this lyric is found in the quiet acknowledgment of the Divine Presence. The poet's journey is nearing its end. This expectation, although it overpowers both his physical and spiritual faculties, is a mystical one. Of the One who will come, his senses will be aware of a single evidence if any: they will merely hear His whisper. But within mind, heart, and soul, the Visitor's action will be most powerful and efficacious. It will mean supreme liberation, it will bring the long-sought *katharsis*—his purification. It will bring forgiveness, security, relief; the past with its darkness and restlessness and agony will be over forever.

For the mature Rebora there can be no more wonderful or

prodigious experience. Very few have been able to describe it with such dignity and immediacy, with such delicacy and beauty. The poet has finally found the right words. Divine grace will soon come to purify his soul but, in a sense, another grace has already touched and purified his tongue. Obscurities so common in other of his poems, crudities so frequent in the past, are no more. All trace of them has disappeared. Now that the conflict has been resolved and peace has descended, the poet has become more articulate.

Religious poetry is perhaps the most difficult and exacting of all types of poetry. And Rebora is to be admired for these verses that indeed mark a lyrical summit in contemporary poetry. Fate, true fate, is upon him. Passion, true passion, makes him flame and burn. Yet, while he conveys to us his tremendous inner delight (one thinks of the spring thaw of northern rivers), he is able, as the great masters are, to tell his story soberly, clearly and simply, almost with detachment, without crowding it with a display of emotions. It is a pianissimo reminiscent of the purest musical melodies.

The images Rebora uses are most common: the lighted room in the surrounding darkness *(l'ombra accesa),* the bell *(il campanello),* the four walls *(le quattro mura)*—and yet, the magic of his poetry transfigures them. The shadow is alight like the eyes of one alert in joyous expectation. The bell spreads a pollen of sound *(polline di suono).* The bare walls are astonished by space *(stupefatte di spazio).* And the refrain repeated again and again, "I wait for no one" *(Non aspetto nessuno),* adds immensely to the setting for the dramatic arrival.

The poet's focus bears lightly and yet strongly on the attentive reader: the face is strained almost painfully *(l'imagine tesa); time* is watched second by second; *sound* is there, too, scattered like pollen by the bell; and *space* with its silent, desertlike immensity. And the poet is alone—for God comes when everything has vanished, when everything has died without and within. Only absolute fullness can fill absolute emptiness.

A mystic might comment that in reality the Guest had already entered the house while the poet was waiting for Him, recalling the thought of Blaise Pascal,[1] "You would not search for me if you had not already found me."[2] He would commend also the description of God, who comes when all is quiet and peaceful and silent *("Non in commotione Dominus"):* God is the one who blossoms unseen; God is forgiveness of sin—and sin (what a sharp definition!) is "that which makes one die"; God will bring awareness of His treasures but He will also make man aware of the preciousness of his soul. With admirable insight into Christian theology, the poet sees God, in His conquest of the poet's soul, as bringing relief both to Himself and to the poet. Rebora does not say that suffering will be wiped out: he speaks only of relief. He knows that suffering will go on but it will no longer be accompanied by despair, but by faith and hope and charity.

No wonder *"Dall'imagine tesa"* has been described as "the finest poem of the *Canti anonimi*,"[3] "Rebora's greatest confession, and one of the most poetic of the century,"[4] "the most sublime lyric of our years."[5]

CHAPTER 13

Mazzini's Disciple

REBORA'S SPIRITUAL ITINERARY DID NOT BEGIN WITH HIS conversion at the age of forty-five. As a young man, while declaring himself a lyricist, not a philosopher, he strove for sanctity as he conceived it—to enrich his life with love, to improve his character, to motivate his actions. He expressed love most sincerely; he delved beyond appearances; he wanted to discover the reason for human sentiments in order to understand eternal reality.

Rebora was not a man of letters *(letterato)*, but a mystic who had, earlier in his life, made Giuseppe Mazzini's cry, *Dio e Popolo*, his own.[1] His mission was to serve *God and the People*, and he believed Mazzini's message that the world was eager to learn of God, to make progress, and to promote unity. Raised in a Mazzinian atmosphere, he had imbibed the sentiments of duty, virtue, love, sacrifice. Rebora could say what Mazzini says of his parents in the dedication of his essay "The Duties of Man": "The republican instincts of my mother taught me to seek out among my fellows the Man . . . and the simple unconscious virtue of my father accustomed me to admire the silent and unnoticed virtue of self-sacrifice."

Clemente Rebora admired Giuseppe Mazzini, the outstanding figure of the *Risorgimento* whose youth had been spent in literary and philosophical studies. After joining the *Carbonari*, he was imprisoned, and went into exile. But Mazzini often came secretly to Italy, although he had been condemned to death *in absentia*. In London in 1858 he founded the newspaper *Pensiero ed azione* (Thought and Action). He supported Garibaldi's expedition to Sicily, but, unlike the latter, remained a confirmed republican and strove for Italian unification.

Mazzini's program was not only political, but deeply social, aiming at human redemption on a religious and moral basis, at liberty and justice. His writings on politics, social science, philosophy, and literature were inspired by his great moral strength.

Throughout Rebora's correspondence one notes his insistence on "Thought and Action" which goes back to Mazzini who wrote in 1861: "Art's special mission is to spur men to translate *thought into action.* . . . The thought dominating an age is almost always . . . contained in it; but it remains sterile, a subject of inert contemplation for the individual, powerless to modify social conditions, to become incarnated in man, to guide his actions. Religion seizes that thought and linking back to heaven, consecrating it with a sanction of divine origin and a future, sets it down as the norm and supreme intent of human actions and thereby transforms the world."

I *Rebora's Mission*

Although Rebora was not successful in his efforts to join the teachers in the program of the National Association for the Mezzogiorno, he was fully aware of his mission in life. To his mother, he wrote: "I have not shut myself in a mean circle, but I have, if it is possible, strengthened certain beliefs of mine which, so far as it will be in my power, I shall never deny."

He was referring to his commitment to go to Reggio Calabria—a commitment which was never fulfilled, through no fault of his, since the teaching position he was to fill did not materialize. He explained to her that the work was a worthy one and in keeping with the ideals of the Italian Risorgimento, inasmuch as it strove for that *unity* of consciousness *(unità di coscienza)* advocated by Mazzini, who was barely beginning to "become living history."[2]

To his friends, disappointed that his trip to Reggio had "gone up in smoke: not because of his will," Rebora confessed: "I would give my physical health, the amiableness and harmony of my ways, and everything in short, in order to be able to act vigorously: I would bless destiny if it remade me lame and mutilated and made up for it with the knowledge of how to get along in life materially and morally, with the ability to realize in the daily routine or in the eternal some part of what boundingly stirs within me."[3]

Writing several months later those sentiments continued to torment him: "I would take stale bread, a lame body, beatings from men in return for a free manifestation of what I feel as truth. . . ." In answer to a friend's advice to rest, he insisted that "to rest is perhaps more cowardly than killing oneself. And I would make myself a handful of bones if my internal ardor could be given concrete form in unremitting, fruitful work, not for me, but for him who waits for me, that is, God through the people. . . . I feel a higher responsibility of which I am an instrument, whereas I cannot face it."[4]

II *Mazzinian World*

Rebora's zeal as a follower of Mazzini may be found in his early poetry, *Frammenti lirici:* "Heedless shy dreams/ here we fight and die:/ the idea is in the doing."[5] His letters to his brother Piero assumed the same prophetic tone. Here is an excerpt from one:

> The *Educator* is God and we must be only the realizers and begin to help to realize Life which awaits all humans in the course of time. For the time being it is already something to be the *Circe of Goodness,* to attract by the spell of loving action all the seafarers that may reach shore, frightened or disoriented, fleeing from the sea of peaceless passions; and to transform the shipwrecked into pilots, the slaves into free men. *Mazzini* [. . .] says: Unfortunately great wars and political revolutions will be necessary in order that through these upheavals minds may be profoundly shaken, be in ferment, and that the tongues of Fire of the Spirit may enter into them everywhere. Then there will open up the road to the grand religious revolution of the *Era of the Holy Spirit,* that is, of the practical realization of the truth, sensed or fondled only as ecstasy, enthusiasm, etc. — as an imposition of a good still and only *selfish,* that is, of a domination (and not *emancipation*); bolshevism and fascism are two *maximums* of negation, *to clear the way for Affirmation.*
>
> Let us remain faithful, come what may, dear Piero—our hour will come, because it will be, and is everyone's hour in the Immortality of Life.[6]

Like Mazzini, Rebora craved for religious and moral unity which would be achieved through education. Mazzini's thoughts inspired him: "The world thirsts for unity"; "democracy tends to unity"; but "discord is everywhere"; and man must seek "a new heaven and a new earth, which may unite in one, in love of God and man, in faith in a common aim, all those, who tossed between fears of the present and doubtings of the future, now stray in intellectual and moral anarchy. . . . We must found moral unity, the Catholicism of humanity"; "the unity of belief that Christ promised for all peoples"; "a unity which binds the sects in one sole people of believers, and on the churches and conventicles and chapels raises the great temple, Humanity's Pantheon, to God."[7]

Mazzini taught that moral principles must be above material ones, altruism above selfishness, humanity above the individual: "We must find an educative principle, to guide men to better things, to teach them constancy in sacrifice, to bind them to their brothers. . . . This principle is Duty. . . . The supreme virtue is sacrifice—to think, work, fight, suffer, where our lot lies, not for ourselves but others, for the victory of good over evil."[8]

III Mazzini's "The Duties of Man"

In his essay on "The Duties of Man," Mazzini enumerates the various spheres of duty. A man's duties begin with himself and his passionate desire for personal holiness. Goodness is the theme of his writings and political aspirations. He was interested in the moral progress of man and humanity: "To draw near to God, purifying our conscience as a temple, sacrificing self for love—this is our mission. To make ourselves better—this is the order of the day, which must be the rule and consecration of our work."[9]

Throughout his writings Mazzini opposed the French Revolution while insisting on the cult of the nation, emphasizing men's duties and enthusiastically speaking of "collective humanity." According to him, humanity manifests itself in nationalities and every people has a particular mission which constitutes its nationality. He advocated a liberal, humanitarian type of nationalism, calling for "the alliance of the peoples in order to work out their mission in peace and love . . . each supporting and profiting by the other's aid."[10]

Although he lived in a Mazzinian world filled with illusion and exaltation, Rebora succeeded in fulfilling his mission as an educator with sincerity and conviction. Later, when he became a member of the *Gruppo d'Azione,* he was invited to write a biography of Mazzini, an assignment which he feared. But he promised that he would try to be his apostle, and would eventually endeavor to express his thoughts about him in writing.

CHAPTER 14

Mystic

REBORA DEDICATED HIMSELF TO SPIRITUAL STUDIES AND TO lectures of a mystical or pseudomystical nature. Once he professed to being "a religious person with no religion," when playfully addressing the Circolo del Convegno and alluding to their motto, "Academicians of no academy" *(Accademici di nulla accademia).*

Rebora's interest in theosophy is recalled in a letter to the author by Cesare Angelini, dated December 14, 1956, in which he wrote: "I knew Rebora in Milan in the distant years of the *Convegno,* when he held disquieting theosophic lectures for the *"belle signore"* (society ladies) creating a suggestive atmosphere by the sudden lowering of his voice and the lights in the lovely rooms painted by Tiepoli in the home of Tommaso Gallarati Scotti."[2]

To those lectures Rebora refers in a letter to his brother Piero: "What is important for me is what must anyhow be fulfilled in me: for signor Clemente Rebora I have neither interest nor any pity whatsoever. I continue privately (besides my various disparate lessons, and my activities, domestic and secret) life-conversations on Tagorian themes, at the Camperio's, before a feminine, but very select public; and I am asked by various parties, directly (and indirectly, by Catholic *mystics,* whom I feel in duty bound to know better). The more I remain hidden, the more they come looking for me. . . ."[3]

With theosophists, Rebora, as a disciple of Mazzini, believed in the universal brotherhood of humanity. He therefore strove to promote theosophy. He wanted to draw together all persons of good will, whatever their opinions, who sought and aspired to truth. With them he held that truth should be sought by study, reflection, purity of life, devotion to high ideals. For Rebora every religion was an expression of Divine Wisdom.

I Tagore

One can readily understand Rebora's enthusiasm for Rabindranath Tagore[4] when he met him in Milan. In his dark robes with his calm, impassive face, arched forehead, white hair reaching to his shoulders and flowing beard, Tagore resembled an ancient sage. His eyes were habitually kept lowered, his voice was thin and gentle. Essentially an ethicist and a conciliator, he worked for social welfare. He was a humanitarian with a strongly mystical tinge with whom Rebora felt a spiritual kinship. During that period, along with oriental mysticism, Rebora became extremely interested in Buddhism and, as a follower of Tagore, even planned on going to the University of Santiniketan in Bengal, India, as is indicated by the following letter to him:

Master, I received with joy your greeting, which you were good enough to entrust to Signora Meyer Camperio, in Prague, last June. It was to me a pledge and spur to better deserve it, by continuing with greater fervor the spiritual work I expect to do to the degree allowed me by my obscurity here in Milan, where I will give this coming fall a "Life Course," taking, as a guideline, the *Sādhanā,* and reverting to your major works, such as are known in Italy. The possibility you caused to flash through my mind, of my being allowed to come then to Santiniketan University, is a high hope for me which I keep alive meanwhile by making myself worthy of it. I would deem it the greatest good fortune if it were given me to assimilate, by your side, the centuries-old human experience of Indian thought, so as to be able later, on my return home, to avail myself of it in the activity of constructive goodness which I already feel as a sweet and irresistible duty. However I lack some necessary requisites for a fruitful stay in your school: among other things I do not know English, although I promise to familiarize myself with it as soon as possible. After that, I should hope to be thoroughly ready in the fall of 1922, a year hence. I am 36 years old and I am free and without any obligation whatsoever. At any rate, with profound and devoted gratitude, I thank you for having been born into the world. Clemente Rebora.[5]

II Janârdana

He never did go to India, but his study of English made in preparation for the trip enabled him to translate *Janârdana,* a mystical tale published anonymously in London in 1905.[6] Rebora's translation, first published in 1922, was republished the following year with a lengthy commentary under the title *Colui che ci esaudisce—Gianardana* (He who hears us—Janârdana).

The artistic purpose of the work is in line with modern Indian literature, while its philosophical structure is based on the asceticism of the Yoga doctrine. It recalls his own spiritual struggles after World War I, and represents his personal quest for God, in the manner of a true mystic. His friends were pleased with the tale and his translation and commentary, and one of them even offered to translate the whole work into French.

Significantly the commentary is preceded by the words of Mazzini: "Each one of us must purify, as a temple, his own soul from all selfishness, face, with a religious sense of the decisive importance of his search, the problem of his own life, listening to his heart's voice, in order to understand and pursue his own mission." *(Ciascuno di noi deve purificare, come tempio, la propria anima da ogni egoismo, collocarsi di fronte, con un senso religioso dell'importanza decisiva della ricerca, al problema della propria vita, ascoltando le voci del cuore, per intendere e seguire la propria missione).*

In the commentary Rebora writes:

> Today in fact . . . it is being realized that the seers of all ages and places alluded, often independently of one another, to the same goal when they pointed out the path to *eternal salvation:* an uphill path both dutiful and irresistible because going up it we notice, as we progressively achieve a higher level, how it is possible to gain gradually a view that is broader and hence real and at one with Life, which it sublimates into a *mission.* And then comes trust of height, for as we strive upward, the doubt of our abyss is converted into certainty of elevation. . . . This is the *religious conversion* toward which we *all* are necessarily headed from the beginning. . . . The substance of *Janârdana* is an inner experience through which, following and believing in the Ideal of Life, the soul *earns* and recognizes its own divine immortality, that is, it is transformed into the reality of Love to which it is destined: and thus feels it can no longer die.[7]

Rebora noted that the author of *Janârdana* "treats of the human soul under the appearance of a woman who discovers God in the man she loves—the Creator in the Creature—perhaps to show how human unity consists precisely in 'man and woman,' who are one single truth in the divine attainment of Life, while divided, they are in effect *divorce* and therefore *death;* and to make us aware that woman today is liberating herself from the subjection under which she necessarily lay when she was conceived or approached as an instrument of reproduction or of pleasure. . . ."[8]

This is the theme he developed in the courses he taught in the 1920s at the Accademia Libera di Cultura ed Arte, at the Circolo Filologico Femminile and at the Scuola Martignoni in Milan. The course title was "Woman and Life." Here, even more than mysticism, one finds that Rebora's association with Mazzinian thought was constant. He worked, he encouraged others, he prayed for the good results of his mission. It is clear, not only from the many letters to his brother Piero and to the Countess Bice Rusconi but also to his friends and to the students who flocked to him for advice, that Rebora's vocation was to help humanity—to educate himself and to educate others, as though he were preparing himself for a great assignment in life.

III Libretti di Vita

Among his missionary activities must be included his editing of a series of spiritual books called *Libretti di Vita*. In the preface to the series, Rebora wrote that it aimed at presenting elements of philosophical and religious education. It consisted of writings which would "emphasize how profitable it is to discover the profound unity of different beliefs rather than confirm the incompatibility of forms which are the transitory point of view of human ascent toward superior syntheses of fellowship."[9] This project does not belong to Rebora's literary activities, but rather to his wandering about in search of truth. It was a new and risky endeavor if one considers the times (1924), the subject matter, and the authors.[10]

In his letter to one of the ladies attending his lectures, a very devout Catholic, he confided his concern about its success and encouraged her to promote the sale of the books. He told her that the publishing house had already been warned that he was "heretical and irreligious."[11]

Always leaning toward Mazzinianism and mysticism, Rebora believed that modern religious revelation was given to us by Mazzini, and by the Polish mystic Towianski, whom he called "the purest guide for understanding life: he has truly read in God. He is the *giver of concrete form* to the eternal truths of the Gospel, and gives us the criterion for *knowing ourselves* and for recognizing in a practical, crystalline and simple way the causes and effects of the actions of individuals and of mankind, in order to establish in us that sense of the Truth (which is after all creation and goodness and *peace*), a sense by saving which we may be saved, or at least may not be left at the mercy of events, but may be sustained in a loving and eternal reason, a reason both *energetic and a transformer* of what seems the 'odd tragicalness' of existence."[12]

IV Political Attitude

Clemente Rebora's efforts may not show any lasting achievement, but his influence was felt in his classes, which attracted women of leisure in particular, owing perhaps to his mysticism, his humility, his warm and persuasive tone. He did not participate in the cultural and political upheaval of the day. Regarding his political tendencies, his brother Piero wrote: "During Fascism,[13] Clemente kept himself completely isolated; he disapproved of many things and admired others, but he distrusted politicians and could not even understand them."[14]

While that is true, it is interesting to note that when duty called, Rebora did not hesitate to make his contribution as citizen and humanitarian. He did not approve of Fascist tactics. On June 20, 1924, he joined other Milan teachers in a written protest formulated by him and sent to the newspapers. It was a "manifesto-letter" *(lettera-manifesto)* entitled "After the Matteotti Crime" *(Dopo il delitto Matteotti),* that is, the murder, on June 10, of Giacomo Matteotti at the hands of Fascist goons.[15]

In 1926, Rebora wrote:

Italy is still to take possession of her task—and the huge powers given her today threaten instead to be directed toward selfish ends, and I know that a shirked mission is atoned for, and all the more sorely the more highly an individual is endowed. Instead of being inspired by our own prophetic tradition which points out our task, our character, the tone of our conscience, we, straying, imitate Germany, England, France, the United States.... *Italy of Humanity:* this is the third mission of Rome—and we cannot live even nationally if we do not live universally; and Europe, and through it the world, will have no peace, so long as the Gordian knot of Rome is not untied: but instead this sublime task assigned to us (if worthy) by Providence, is diverted by Cupiditas, by the imperialisms of pope and king in veiled struggle one against the other.[16]

Such was Rebora's political idea: before his conversion he desired a universal Rome, to preach the Gospel of Mazzini. After it, he sought only to preach the Gospel of Christ, while still striving as always to become "Italian in order to be human, and be human in order to be divine."[17]

CHAPTER 15

The Road to Damascus

> The mountain hopes while rising to the sky:
> and it is first in sunlight, wind, and frost.
> Even so does hope in Christ make
> pure hearts fearless through the cross to glory.
> (Clemente Rebora, *Hope*)

EVEN THOUGH CLEMENTE REBORA'S DOCTORAL DISSERTATION WAS on the philosopher Romagnosi, it was not to philosophy but to poetry and to theosophy that he dedicated whatever free time his duties as a secondary-school teacher spared him. When his teaching proved too distracting, he gave it up to devote himself entirely to spiritual pursuits, which eventually led to his conversion to the Catholic faith and the Christian idealism of Antonio Rosmini (1797 - 1855), whose order he joined in 1931.

Like other writers of the early twentieth century, Rebora used religious terminology to express a nebulous, pedagogical, and political morality. Although he was an outsider in politics, he had the correct perception of the political situation and of the base morality of the times. His letters furnish us with the confirmation that everything he wrote—biographical annotations, historical and cultural references, his obvious existentialism[1]—was secondary in importance. One realizes that the key to his correspondence was a truly religious spirituality. Pregnant with prophetic insights, all his writings have a continuity that can be translated into Grace, the Divine Presence he refers to implicitly in the lyrical poem *"Dall'Imagine Tesa,"* the last poem of his *Canti anonimi*.[2]

A further confirmation of this spirituality came from his brother Piero in a letter to Giuseppe Prezzolini:

I wish to note only that Clemente's conversion was not at all of an intellectual nature. Intellect and culture have never taken hold of his soul. His spiritual ascent was only a tragic rebellion against human society, almost against life itself; a life which he found shameful, vulgar, stupid, without meaning. This view of his has something in common with my immense surprise that men do not commit suicide. His road to Damascus was a road of desperation; but on it, through a series of singular revelations, Clemente found Truth, Certainty, *i.e.,* the immortality of the soul, eternal life, the law of love given by a Supreme Being; in short, Faith.[3]

I *Lectures*

In 1928, at the Milan *Lyceum,* Rebora gave a series of lectures on "Women and the Religion of Rome." He was pressured into giving a final lecture which would be a preview of the course to be given the following year on "Christ and Women." But in preparing for this lecture, he found the topic more difficult than he had anticipated, and did not feel sure of himself. The day came and he began by reading an ancient text on the Scillitan[4] Martyrs. Among the twelve martyrs giving eloquent testimony of faith and courage before the Consul Saturnius, five were women. In an effort to absolve them from the accusation of being Christians and set them free, the judge said: " 'Are you out of your minds?' One martyr replied: 'We fear no one but the Lord God who is in Heaven.' The trial continued. Vestia said: 'I am a Christian.' " On reading that one by one during the trial, each had said, "I am a Christian," Rebora's vision blurred. He hesitated. He made an effort to continue reading, but it was useless. Something tightened in his throat. He put his head between his hands, unable to go on. There was complete silence. The audience was shocked and, as he got up to leave, they thought he was sick from excessive work.

II *Seeking Truth*

Trembling, Rebora walked through the streets of Milan, oblivious of all that surrounded him. He felt alone, obsessed by a burning search for God. Perhaps it was as he looked up at the Madonnina of the Duomo of Milan that he felt his search had ended. He tells us in the *Curriculum Vitae* that through Mary he found his God:

> It was Our Lady who took me by the hand,
> compassionately she brought me to her ardent Son
> to the happy suffering of Christ
> that transfigures life down here
> into the beginning of eternal love,
> free gift, complete: now, or never more.
> Even less than a drop is enough,
> I need
> all the Blood of Christ.

To his friend, Adelaide Coari, Rebora expressed a desire to discuss his dilemma with Cardinal Ildefonso Schuster. But it was not easy to be received by His Eminence, who had just recently become Archbishop of Milan. She sought help from Monsignor Angelo Giuseppe Roncalli (the Apostolic Visitator to Bulgaria who later became His Holiness, Pope John XXIII). He was acquainted with Rebora's works—having received from Adelaide Coari the translation of *Gianardana*—and immediately arranged for a meeting between the poet and the cardinal.

Confirming this meeting with the cardinal on October 22, 1929, Adelaide Coari told him that Rebora was a fervent soul, a good poet and writer; he had been raised in a family of extreme rectitude, but atheistic; he had been hostile to the Church, which he considered an obstacle to the religious life. She added that during the last two years he began to doubt his beliefs and sought the truth about the Church. She assured the cardinal that only he could help Rebora make a decision. In fact, Rebora recalls this visit of October 24 in his diary. His Eminence insisted that he make a decision. He told him he could no longer remain at the threshold of the Church: it would be equivalent to being five hundred thousand kilometers away. He also advised him to seek a priest as spiritual director. The poet left the meeting confused. But three days later he went to the Duomo and, for the first time, he was able to genuflect spontaneously and make the Sign of the Cross.

God's grace finally reached Rebora. His correspondence at that time reveals that his conversion was imminent, as shown by the fact, for example, that in May 1928 he was looking forward to meeting his brother Piero to hear from him of his "loyal search for the Love that moves the Sun and the other Stars," outside of which "all is *vanitas vanitatum*" and the devil's own flour that turns to bran. And he goes on:

We are called to become *heirs* of the Roman spirit and of Catholicism, which keep Action and Thought, to go from Roma (Rome) to Amor (Love) [AMOR—anagram of ROMA] (when Rome becomes the heart of the Humanity of God it will be rebaptized Amor. . .) . I know that, although they [Keyserling's works] are an indication of the divine exigency impelling us toward the fullness of time, they also indicate false images of good, as do all the new Indo-American-German-Anglo-Saxon religions, as well as the neomagic and neopagan ones: because all place God at the service of the "Ego" (the "Ego" of person, of belief, of nation, of humanity, etc.) proposing terrestrial or cosmic ends that fall into the closed circle of the world, finite, destitute and fallacious. I, since I was twenty up until now, have tried *all* the directions: and I have found them deceitful, except the one pointed out by Mary and Jesus; and if I do not belong visibly to the Church, since I am an exile in my homeland, that is due only to previous debts that perhaps I am close to having paid off, and even more to my mission, as I try to understand it, in my almost uninterrupted prayer. And the moment my position should appear mistaken to me and I should feel I must visibly join the Church, and therefore my Homeland and the Homeland of Homelands, in the ways presently practiced, I would do it singing without a single regret or doubt in the world. . . .[5]

III *Conversion*

And six months later he exultingly wrote to his brother Piero: "I am now grounded in God, and through Mary and Jesus, and the saints, visible and invisible, I draw eternal life to conquer what remains of Adam in me and around me, toward the manifestation in preparation for centuries of centuries. I can do nothing more on my own, but something I can if I start all over again from God."[6]

Finally, on November 24, feast of St. John of the Cross, he entered the Catholic Church, living in solitude under the direction of a Rosmini Father.

To prepare for his departure, after asking his sister Marcella to help herself to his furniture, he opened all the drawers, pulled out books he would not need in the seminary, emptied his desk of all papers, letters, etc. One can imagine Rebora surrounded by these things, perhaps seated on his bed with scraps of paper, old photographs, souvenirs from the war, countless items which reminded him of his past. Though filled with friendships and joys, he recalled that during these years he did not enjoy the one true friendship—that of God. He must have vividly recalled certain periods of the past with its pleasures, its hopes, its bonds

The Road to Damascus

that seemed indissoluble. Filled with regret, he pulled out an old sack into which he placed the torn items, stuffing into it his manuscripts and a large part of his papers, all his letters, critical studies, books on religion, philosophy, literature, music. He destroyed everything he had held so dear and then prayed silently. Suddenly he heard the voice of the ragman yelling on the street. And, as Rebora tells us in the *Curriculum Vitae,* he called him to his apartment to dispose of his sack. Deliberately, definitely, he broke all ties with his former way of life.

> Love loved back, Love wants all.
> And came the day, that in divine fury
> the truth of Christ constrained me
> to execute books and writings and papers:
> and that surely was some tearing up!
> When what was most of my evil
> was reduced to a shredded heap,
> I felt light in happy freedom.
> And lo! suddenly up to me
> from the bottom of the street uproar
> came a pathetic cry well-known to me:
> Rags . . . —Hey, rag-picker! —He tramps up
> the steps one by one to the top,
> loads the sack on his yoke:
> for a few cents took the mess away.
> The city lights going on that evening
> found me alone thinking of the past:
> my soul, placed in the eternal,
> was seized perhaps by melancholy, but not by sadness.

Cardinal Schuster of Milan received him with paternal interest and understanding and arranged for his future with the Rosmini Fathers at Domodossola.

Before taking any steps, feeling his unworthiness, he withdrew to pray and to meditate. He was looked upon with suspicion by many of his former friends, who could not believe that the Rebora they knew had been converted. Rebora's letters after his conversion invoked a spirit of quiet meditation. They were his contribution to the spiritual life of the friends to whom he wrote. With Paul he could say: "I press on towards the goal, to the prize of God's heavenly calling in Christ Jesus."

Rebora followed Cardinal Schuster's advice faithfully and, although the diocesan seminary in Venegono did not consider him a suitable candidate for ordination to the secular priesthood, he was accepted into the religious order of the Rosmini Fathers on May 23, 1931, at Domodossola. After two years of Novitiate he made his profession of faith to His Eminence, whom he addressed as: "My first and beloved and unforgettable Shepherd" *(Mio primo e amato e indimenticabile Pastore)*. Thereafter he continued to keep him informed, asking his prayers and blessing as he took each step—minor orders—to ordination. Full of gratitude he acknowledged that "from you I received my first decision, my first Holy Communion, my Confirmation, and your blessing to enter Religion; from your *Liber Sacramentorum* I obtained so much good."[7] Clemente Rebora made his religious profession on May 13, 1933, and was ordained a priest on September 19, 1936.

Rebora's conversion was genuine. It was a clarification of his moral commitment to his fellow man. The attraction he felt for everything noble, his many friends who prayed for his return to the faith[8]—all moved him to seek fulfillment of his ideals in Catholicism.

Unlike Paul's conversion on the way to Damascus, Rebora's was the result of a long search through the highways and byways of religious and pseudoreligious thought. Perhaps the women, the mystical Catholic women who attended his lectures, may have had something to do with his final conversion, just as Lucia did with the conversion of the Innominato.[9]

CHAPTER 16

Canti dell'infermità

IN 1955, AFTER SOME THIRTY YEARS OF SELF-IMPOSED SILENCE, Rebora resumed his singing with *Canti dell'infermità*. He could no longer offer the Sacrifice of the Altar but, from his sickbed, he offered the Sacrifice of the Cross. His solitude, his sufferings, his humiliations—all became a prayer. He was *"semivivo"* (semi-alive), as he later described himself when he sent a copy of *"Gesù il Fedele"* to the Archbishop of Milan, Giovanni Battista Montini, His Holiness, Pope Paul VI.

Rebora revealed the dark night of his soul in the poem "How fearful to return" *(Terribile ritornare a questo mondo):*

> How fearful to return to this world
> when already all fibers
> were straining
> to cross over!
> And my body refuses me all service,
> and my soul no longer finds its beginning.
> Every divine command is a black effort.
> All goes thoughtlessly:
> the abyss calls out to the abyss.

The last line is not a cry of despair but a sad supplication as the abyss of misery invokes the abyss of mercy.

Throughout the lyric fragments the power of verbal sound is used, and words become charged with new meaning. There is a directness and purity of language, a return to the essence of the word, a kind of shock treatment on words to restore their freshness and impact.

In his poetry Rebora is interested only in giving expression to his innermost feelings. His words do not follow a pattern of linguistic elegance. He mixes them at random and one finds words that are common, different, classical, baroque, rare, humble, melodious, harsh. He places dignified words next to vulgar ones. There are words from the Lombard and Tuscan dialects. Besides words that are rarely used, he prefers rare variants in the spelling of certain words both in his prose and in his poetry.

Figures of speech are frequently used in the *Canti dell'infermità:* alliteration, metaphors, personification abound. His work manifests a dissatisfaction with expression shown by a constant play on words and by the use of words that often assume a mystic flavor.[1]

The *Canti dell'infermità* are Rebora's poetic and spiritual testament, as he himself says at the beginning of the volume: "Poetry has become for me, more than ever, a concrete way to love God and my brothers. *Charitas lucis, refrigerium crucis"* (The charity of the light, the comfort of the cross).

Toward the end of his life the thought of his poetry filled him with anxiety and fear. Had he been too pleased with his poetic contributions? Had he been more interested in the "poet" rather than in the "Christian"? On December 30, 1955, Rebora wrote a "Prelude to the *Canti dell'infermità:" (Preludio ai Canti dell'infermità):*

> If the sun shines outside without You inside,
> all ends, smothered in dark fog.
> What desperate horror, my Jesus,
> to find at the end that I only sang the ego!
>
> If to go up a poet, but not as a saint,
> to lose even one single point of Your love,
> oh! take from me all singing vein,
> without saying more, taken up in Your voice!

I *Spiritual Itinerary*

Poetry was Rebora's *itinerarium,* that is, the way to understand and resolve the conflicts that tortured him during his spiritual search. *Canti dell'infermità* is the continuation of his early poetry. It remains meditation, concept, truth. His destruction, at the moment of conversion, of all his manuscripts and a large portion of his annotated library, was dictated by a

Canti dell'infermità

resolve to dedicate himself to important work for humanity. His artistic vocation was converted to a religious vocation, and there was no longer need to repeat the desires expressed in his early poetry. Now there is a deep pang, almost a secret remorse, which is finally resolved in the poem "Hope" *(Speranza)*[2]

> The sea hopes for the shore wave after wave:
> but once there, each wave breaks up and vanishes.
>
> Even so does human hope delude itself,
> and in the end comes to cruel disappointments.
>
> The mountain hopes while rising to the sky
> and it is first in sunlight, wind and frost.
>
> Even so does hope in Christ make
> pure hearts fearless through the cross to glory.

II Notturno

With the permission of his superiors, Rebora privately made a vow in June 1936 always to ask for "the grace to suffer and to die obscure, pulverized in the love of Christ" *(La grazia di patir, morire oscuro, polverizzato nell'amor di Cristo)* —words he repeated in 1955 in his poem "Nocturne" *(Notturno)* —a poem which portrays the Christian and saintly Rebora. Now, close to death, suffering the dark night of the senses and the soul, he feels that he has not achieved the sanctity and love that fidelity to his vow should have brought. It is from this state of anxiety and tension that the poem, *"Notturno,"* is born.

> My blood yearns for Jesus who sets on fire.
> *Burn me!* I say: but my word is empty.
> *Save me all crucified* (I cry)
> *bloody with your blood!* But a nail in the wall,
> I am sunk into physical miseries.
> The grace to suffer, to die obscure,
> pulverized in the love of Christ:
> to be manure in His vineyard,
> a floor that is walked on, and forgotten,
> a pedal pressed so that deep
> may rise the organ's voice in the temple—

and prove in the end a useless servant:
this, Jesus, you demanded of me, and vainly
did I promise, if then I turn souls away.

During this mystical experience, Rebora's hope is renewed. The poem continues, invoking Mary, who assures him of God's mercy:

'Tis beautiful to offer, like flowering to the flower:
but the deed is other than dreamed.
Father, Father who still keep me down here,
grant that in me the *Ecce* be not lost or weakened!
In the meantime I am dying because I cannot die.
My blood burns, Jesus sets on fire:
if it does not burst into flame, it is only heat.
I invoke Mary who is the Flame of the Fire;
her face benign, she seems to say firmly:
—Penance, my son, penance:
pray with a prayer that may see no effect:
always offer yourself, even if the offer is vain;
and while you live uncertain of your lot,
humbled, and like one accursed,
God confirms you in mercy.

Every season of Rebora's life is full of wonders. In the *Canti dell'infermità* one notes his burning energetic zeal, his scrupulous strictness of life, his implicit obedience to what he considered God's will. Faith meant *to live God* within himself; to see and receive the divine superreality into his own existence. It was a divine illumination of reality, not an escape from reality. It was a leap into the yet unknown. It was a risk, a gamble.

After penetrating into Rebora's spiritual but very real world following the disillusionment and disgust of World War I, and after searching out the thoughts that animated and characterized his entire life, one is confronted with difficult thoughts in a difficult language. Yet it is possible to understand him and to establish a spiritual affinity. He gives us a sense of reality, as true as that of the senses and of the imagination: the reality of sin and death, of redemption and grace, of expectation and resurrection, the reality of Christ and of God.

Each poem of the *Canti dell'infermità* is, above all, a prayer—simple, humble, supplicating. At times, it is inspira-

Canti dell'infermità

tional; at times, mystical. Always it is the story of Rebora's spiritual itinerary.

CHAPTER 17

Curriculum Vitae

TOWARD THE END OF HIS LIFE, REBORA, A VICTIM OF arteriosclerosis, resumed writing verse. The younger generation did not fail to recognize its purity and depth. In fact, on October 7, 1956, he received the "Cittadella" Award, given annually to a poet, for his long autobiographical poem, *Curriculum Vitae*. It was a formal acknowledgment of the place he deserves in the Italian literature of this century.

Diego Valeri, representing the Committee which selected Rebora for the award, expressed the opinion of the literary world when he recalled that Rebora, from the days of *La Voce* to that day, had followed a very difficult path in obedience to his own need for direct and full expression. His poetry is, according to Valeri, "a fatiguing and painful expression of an intimate perpetual drama, alternating mystical enthusiasm and human bewilderment. . . . It is very true that such a moral irresistible and religious need ends up sometimes by disturbing the formal harmony of his work, but it is likewise true, that, in the end, from the clash and deep conflict, the poetic word expressed is filled with human meaning and richer with spiritual light."[1]

I *Autobiographical Poem*

Rebora began writing his *Curriculum,* which he claimed "is not a complete biography, but only a poetic need," in June of 1955, the month Catholics dedicate to the Sacred Heart. Having finished it during July, dedicated to the Precious Blood of Christ, Rebora made reference to the *"perfetta Regola"* ("As I was put in order by the perfect Rule") of the Institute of Charity founded by Antonio Rosmini, whom he called *"quel sapiente"* (that sage), and alluded to the religious beliefs in the old

Tridentine[2] liturgy—the Trinity, Redemption, etc.—which he held so dear:

> The tenderness of the divine Heart,
> which descends from the Trinitarian mystery,
> I, who had been living for nine lusters
> but had had life for barely two years,
> remade an infant in the school of the Living One.
> And by Heaven I was entrusted to that sage
> who, a great genius, annihilated himself in Christ
> so that only His Power might change all.
> As I was put in order by the perfect Rule,
> my dislocated bones found their places:
> my intelligence discovered the first gift:
> the word worked as does light for the eye,
> almost air for my breathing His forgiveness:
> Jesus Love was pregnancy in me.
> Joyful play in forms austere,
> [with me] every day more of a novice to Paradise,
> my sorrow rises and tenderness descends:
> without Confiteor there is no going up to the Altar,
> the Magnificat concludes the Miserere
> and the De profundis rises into the Te Deum.

In his *Curriculum* Rebora tells us that, though his health is declining and his Calvary has begun, divine grace and prayer assist him. While waiting for God he calls to mind whatever in his life relates to Him who grants us pardon in order to give Himself to us. Everything else is to be completely forgotten. Briefly he mentions several facts of his early life: how he disliked being in a *"gonnellino"* (smock), how someone at school using bad words passed him an obscene picture, how growing strong midst uproar and quarrels, his mother used to excuse all his mischief.

He recalls the refrain of an early poem entitled *"Anima Errante,"* ("Alone, wandering and tired/ A soul was drifting"). As a child he could not understand his loneliness, but now he knows why: the absence of Christ in his life. And he remembers some youthful fantasies and musings. One day, although ignorant of religion, he was struck by the meaning of the Latin name *Clemens,* repeating its syllables backwards: *ens, mens, Clemens.* Inspired by the meaning of each syllable, he made up his *mind* to be *clement* for the rest of his life and consciously aimed at achieving "goodness," a goal making him worthy of the name and unconsciously bringing him closer to the "mystery of God":

> *Ens Mens Clemens,* mystery of God,
> Father, Son and Holy Spirit,
> eternal life: and goodness only is life.

II *Parish Priest*

On June 12, 1957, Rebora was asked during an interview: "Is it true, Father, that, once you became a Rosmini Father, you did not want to speak of poetry, or hear anyone speak of your poetry, as though it were wrong to speak of it?" "No!" he answered resolutely. "It is not true! I did not speak of poetry because there was something more important to do."[3]

And indeed from the moment of his conversion Rebora was absorbed in the desire to unite himself to God. As he progressed in his spiritual life, he enjoyed the consolations of permanent union with God and, engulfed in bodily miseries, he experienced also the torments of spiritual abandonment.

While in Rovereto, where he performed various duties as a parish priest, Rebora agreed, in obedience to his superiors, to have his brother Piero edit a new edition of all his poetry. When asked for a résumé of his life, he answered that he was sending some brief notes, written hurriedly, which were necessary to justify the publication of his poetry for the glory of God and the good of souls, in times when one had to be with Christ, or with the anti-Christ, adding that one day his mother told him: "You are a priest and belong to a religion which still does not exist."[4] And if friends spoke of the importance of his poetry, he would say that "the Clemente Rebora of the past was dead and buried." He would also remind them that the experience of a lifetime must promote one's salvation and lead "to the One who is the Way, the Life and the Truth."

With regard to the information he had sent, Rebora soon became very concerned. He felt a growing repugnance that there should be a biographical sketch which was not his "obituary." He told his brother to contact the superior of the Rosmini Fathers for authorization to publish it, strongly doubting that approval would be granted since permission had been received for the reprint of the poems only. He insisted that information on "such delicate matters," unfortunately, had been thrown together in a hurry and needed revision "for the sake of truth and honesty."

Shortly after, on July 1, 1946, Rebora informed his brother Piero that his verses were not written *currenti calamo*—dashed off—(with the exception of rhymes that just flowed in the first rough draft): but there was much work entailed in stripping them of nonessentials (reducing them to the "minimum") that continued almost in his sleep. He added, moreover, that after joining the Rosmini Fathers he wrote a few poems "in obedience to my Superiors." Among those poems were two *(Mater Clementissima, La Chiesola dello Spielberg)* inspired by Silvio Pellico's[5] poems. These were added to the six religious ones he had written since 1936. Hence his reference to the "trickle of water poured from a pail into his literary torrent long since dried up," and the rejection of all his publications.

He hoped his brother intended to limit the biographical sketch to his "literary activity (if that you can call what was first a longing search for *Him* in order *to live);* because otherwise one should at least touch on the immense indescribable travail of my being like a fish gasping on the shore of the divine ocean,[6] and my attempt to jump in unaided—as isolated as I was spiritually—plunging instead into an atrocious putrid joy when about twenty-nine years of age; then the most merciful Hand that gradually pulled me out and finally pushed me into living water to wriggle. . . ."

He recalled that among his lyrics there was *"Movimenti di poesia,"* which ends with *"e verso un richiamo di donna/ impietrandosi, finì/ in una lussuosa Madonna"* (attracted by the thought of woman/ steeling himself, stopped/ at a sensuous Madonna). These words weighed heavily upon his conscience because he considered the poem "a wretched composition" he would have liked to "turn to ashes." In a letter to Piero, he wrote: "Oh Piero, I have never written such a long letter, especially since I consecrated myself to the Lord, and about things which concern me more than Him, and with the difficulty I have in writing: it seems so strange. May God make it truly do some good for souls for the glory of our Everygood! We are in moments in which God asks strength of many of us to save our brothers by dying rather than by merely writing and preaching.'"[7]

III Le Poesie

After years of silence with regard to Clemente Rebora's poetry, the literary world took notice when the collection *Le Poesie* (1913 - 1947) was published,[8] as did a young scholar, Mario Costanzo, who stated that Rebora's poetry and spiritual itinerary had left him bewildered and made him suddenly "resolve a lot of things, and dismantle certain rebellious conceits of a young literary man and, in short, have helped me in my return to the faith."

While Rebora was surprised and moved, he still feared that some passages in the publication might hurt others. The thought caused him indescribable anguish. In fact, his joy turned to sorrow when he began to realize that just as that young man had dug out a 1914 poem of his, *"Prima del sonno,"* and republished it, so too others could bring to light the verses he had rejected with much sadness and shame, which had been eliminated from the volume *Le Poesie*. Aside from his embarrassment, Rebora was concerned that those verses would be harmful to such "noble consciences and young consciences at that." His letter to that young friend confirmed his anxiety:

> I confess to you that your letter gave me much joy because of the dear enthusiasm of your soul and on learning that the poetry of my "itinerary" helped you to return to the faith. Just think, when the volume edited by my brother came out, I went through moments of inexpressible anguish because certain expressions were somewhat blasphemous (and I had been so told) and I was afraid that others might prove somehow harmful to souls (I had previously refused to have republished certain verses that I recalled with sorrow and shame): to do harm to my brothers when I had in the light of grace reached the religious life, and even more, the priesthood! Now I kiss the ground to thank the merciful Lord who chose instead to use them for His own good.[9]

Several years later, in response to his brother Piero's encouraging words about his poetry, Rebora agrees with him about "its efficacy on one's inner life, almost like a vehicle of the invisible into the invisible, and finally a throb of the only reality, the infinite being, of Love, that is God, so that 'God may be all in all' (i *Cor.* XV); but it is also true that one cannot express it [poetry] if it is not given to us: 'I am one who, when Love inspires . . .' [Dante . . .]; now, in my little way, I experience the same effect; but, just as there is spiritual aridity, so I suffer instead poetic aridity. Forgive me, therefore, if I cannot meet your kind expectation; I don't do it purposely; in fact, it would be for me a profound and gushing gratification."[10]

This was the period prior to Rebora's *Curriculum Vitae,* when little or none of his verse had appeared. As for poetry, there is much of it in his correspondence, as one readily sees in another letter to Piero in which he speaks of the initiative of his Florentine artist-friend Primo Conti and others to have readings of his poetry.

What sign of my activity and "present voice" could I send you other than the sign of my daily ministry, in the lyrical invocation to have the grace of loving back Love, Jesus, pulverizing myself in his work among the brothers [his fellow Rosminiani] to our Father who is in Heaven? And to be patient if, as in art, in this Art of arts (aiming to edify souls in the Mystic Body of Christ in eternal life) for me is to fail at every moment? And rejoice at the same time whenever the instant present in the adorable Will of God manages to coincide with His eternal present?

I think further that your meeting to enjoy poetry together as a Catholic community is a manifestation of faith in supernatural values, a yearning towards the total Christ, loving in order to be in the life that does not die—and almost a way of making poetry together, in the tone and rhythm of *Ecce quam bonum et quam jucundum habitare fratres in Unum* ("Behold how good and how joyful it is to dwell as brothers in One"). For this morning I seemed to sense—while I was in thanksgiving after the Holy Mass, when sometimes the Blood of Christ is still coursing through my heart in keeping with *Fluminis impetus laetificat Civitatem Dei* (The force of the river gladdens the City of God) —that poetry, essentially after the Living One, infinite Love, became a creature, consists in discovering and establishing proprieties, references, and concordances between Heaven and earth as well as within and between us; and expressing haltingly the intimate harmony constituted by one substance in Three Persons and Divinity, one with humanity in the Incarnate Word and Christ's members identical with Jesus just as He is with the Father; and resulting in the course of time in a salient aspiration of the created universe, which needs to spiral upwards from the mineral kingdom to the vegetable and from the vegetable to the animal and from the animal to the human, to us incorporated in the Son of God until one day we can—if we stay together as do shoots with the vine—dwell forever in the ineffable fire of love which is the bosom of the Most Holy Trinity through the divine motherhood of imparadised Mary.

Poetry . . . —totally, that is, catholicly understood—is beauty revealing, as a mysterious echo, infinite Goodness, which has such great arms. . . . It derives somewhat from grace (if there has been real inspiration) and hence annihilation of the old man to make us better, more of one mind, trustfully reliant on the Providence of our Celestial Father and unified with the crucified and forsaken Son: desirous of effectuating—as exiles but already fellow-citizens of the Homeland of Light, and running to meet the Groom that has come, is coming, and will come—one heart and one soul in brotherly love which is also loving justice. So that *as we come out of a poetry reading* (and here mention should be made also of the other arts, each one with its sublime gift, and of music as well which in the great musicians is almost a gift of love) we might feel better encouraged to the good and the eternal, prizing again Saint Paul's words: "And in doing good let us not grow tired; for in due time we shall reap if we do not relax. Therefore, while we have time, let us do good to all men, but especially to those who are of the household of faith" (Galatians 6: 9 - 10).[11]

Refusing to compromise and disdaining the social and political trends inspired by rhetoricians and academicians of the early twentieth century, Rebora aimed through his poetry to reach the very roots of his fellow man's problems and his own. He was deeply pleased when the *Curriculum Vitae* won the "Cittadella" Award, pleased for the burden of his poem rather than for its art. After many years of deep anguish and concern about the effect of his early poetry on people, his work was finally acknowledged for its spiritual impact and meaning.

IV *Commissioned Poetry*

Several poems were "commissioned." In 1954, at the request of a young editor, Gianni Scheiwiller, Rebora collaborated with thirty Italian poets. Asked to send even "one line," he was told that his participation, as a priest, in the collection, honoring Rimbaud[12] on the one hundredth anniversary of his birth, would be meaningful. He wrote the poem *"Poesia e Santità* (Poetry and sanctity) for the occasion:

> While creation ascends in Christ to the Father,
> in our dark lot
> all is birth throe:
> how much dying to bring forth life!
> yet the children of only one Mother, who is divine,
> happily see the light:
> life that love produces with tears,
> and, if it yearns, here below is poetry;
> but only holiness completes the song.

Curriculum Vitae

In 1955, Scheiwiller, the young editor, requested a poem for a collection of poetry in honor of Ezra Pound,[13] which was published in an effort to obtain his freedom from political imprisonment. Referring to Dante's *Divine Comedy,* Rebora repeated, as he had frequently in the past, one of his favorite verses: "Love that moves the sun and other stars" *(L'amor che muove il sole e l'altre stelle).*

> From eternal Poetry Dante comes to us
> to encourage onto his track art
> which, if true, lifts to true living.
> He sees people who run without goal,
> a human mixture, both isolated and divided:
> Is it hell? Is it purgatory? The world
> looks for Paradise while fleeing it,
> it forces the cage of this universe . . .
> Dante advances in the hubbub that bores him:
> all alone he repeats only one verse:
> *Love that moves the sun and other stars.*
> No one listens . . . but he encounters a squad
> of those whom God destines to elevate
> into supreme beauty both hearts and minds:
> everyone compliments him for his Comedy . . .
> —And now (they say) what are you working on?

While Rebora's poetry was still spontaneous and rich with inspiration, his health was gradually declining. Through bitter sufferings, both physical and spiritual, he rose to closer union with God and his fellow men. In Stresa, on November 1, 1957, death came as more than a liberation for Rebora—it was the beginning of eternal communion with God.

CHAPTER 18

Correspondence

WHAT EXPLAINS THE INTERRELATIONS THAT BIND REBORA'S LYRICS to his prose writing and his correspondence is the fact that he was being himself in all his writings. In both prose and poetry one can recapture and recreate the most important events and more salient episodes of his life, from his childhood at home in Milan to his illness and death in a religious house in Stresa. In his letters he reveals his life as a student, his friendships, his associaton with *La Voce,* his life as a soldier in World War I, his work as a teacher, lecturer, and writer, his conversion to the Catholic faith, and his last years as a priest and member of the Rosmini religious community.

Rebora's letters help us understand his inner life. Not written for publication, but with the sincere belief that they would never serve any purpose other than to communicate with friends, the letters, for their conversational warmth and revealing confidences in the spirit of the day, bring us a breath of the life of his soul. Furthermore, they can be interesting to others in that they reveal a different world—an honestly human, profoundly lived world.

One does not find a wealth of external happenings, but almost a symphony by a complex, sorrowful, ardent, changing spirit; a human heart that has the rare courage to confess, without too much literary simulation, to reveal itself to its very depths without vanity, to express the dramatic, daily complexities of life.

Throughout the letters one sees Rebora in all his sincerity, as his self-evaluation reveals the psychological torture he had experienced, almost like a diary, written hurriedly at times and under all kinds of circumstances.

For example, in a letter to Antonio Banfi, he mentions that he has written seven letters, despite the fact that he is dazed from a sleepless night spent on a derailed train that did not move for five hours: ". . . a marvelous night, pained cries of a hurt passenger, the goodness and nastiness of travelers cheated of their sleep, and all around a great hubbub with outcries of strong engines without a road." In the midst of this chaos, what does Rebora do but "set to music in my mind an unwritten unwritable poem that violently took possession of my nerves and blood."[1]

Rebora was constantly expressing his innermost sentiments, for he needed to confide the ups and downs of his state of mind to someone. There was an impelling need to write, to feel himself united to his fellow man, to participate in sufferings and joys, to help people, to sustain the weak, to enlighten the young, always to do good.

Perhaps one can say that there are passages in Rebora's letters which recall Leopardi's *Zibaldone*—its verbal profusion, passion, existential inquietude. Notwithstanding his antiintellectual and anticultural protests, his letters form an indispensable document in recreating the ideals and attitudes of Italian youth immediately preceding the First World War. Rebora suffered, as few suffered, the moral and intellectual crisis, the anguish, the emptiness that accompanied the wòrld tragedy which was followed by Fascism in Italy.

His friendships definitely influenced both his prose and his poetry, as his letters amply show. His entire correspondence embraces a period of over sixty years with members of his family, his students, and countless friends. Besides those already mentioned in the preceding chapters, there are many letters to Bruno Furlotti,[2] Francesco Meriano,[3] and Bice Rusconi.[4] These friendships began in 1917 and extended to 1930, that is, during the period marked by mysticism and Mazzinianism. They reveal reciprocal understanding and deep affection, as well as dependence on Rebora. They are rare examples of a literary kinship which was permeated with human interests and love.

I *Mombello Hospital*

Correspondence with the artist Bruno Furlotti dates back to World War I. He was a conscientious objector and requested, in 1917, to be executed rather than to be sent to the battlefield. Instead he was admitted to the Mombello Hospital (Milan), where he met Clemente Rebora, who was recuperating from the horrors of war on Mount Podgora. It was to Furlotti that Rebora turned to design the cover for the *Libretti di Vita* series of philosophical works he edited, and it was to Rebora that Furlotti turned to help sell some of his paintings when he was in dire need of financial assistance.

When Burno Furlotti was desperate because his dreams of love did not materialize, it was Rebora who sought to comfort him. Gently he tells him that his *"sin* is great and such because you feel it, because there is in you something so beautiful and healthy that can judge you (though abhorring doing so) as ugly and sick." He urges him to leave town immediately, in a maximum of suffering, and go to the tip end of Italy, ". . . or come to me, to let your torment calm down and see what you have left, what is reborn or dead in you. *Later,* you can pass judgment on yourself and see life or death, as the thing for you, in a sincere and calm mood. The *blotch* causing gangrene in your body and soul you are atoning for right now because of your sense of nausea and of martyrdom. . . . If you kill your soul now, you will not be purified in death, but you will seal in it the blotch causing you shame." With words of encouragement about "dreams and ideals" which can never be achieved, he tells Furlotti that he is waiting for his visit so that together they may decide how, when and where he will go, confessing that he too had experienced moments of desperation when "one terrible night of war and tempest, I was left hugging the sheer drop of a mountain, convinced I would inescapably die there; at dawn, a few feet away, I noticed a darling path that hid and cradled me in the valley."[5]

II La Brigata

Rebora's correspondence with Francesco Meriano was of a different nature and may be compared to Rilke's[6] *Letters to a Young Poet.*[7] There is in them an unusual lack of rhetoric, rare in literary friendships, and an authentic evaluation of current events—war, sickness, love, literary currents. Besides assuring Meriano of his deep affection, he praised his review *La Brigata,* which because of its honesty, was the only contemporary organ that inspired confidence, and therefore he was not ashamed to contribute to it. Speaking of its last issue (February-March

1917), Rebora says that it was shaping up, even though some articles were out of tune. He particularly admired Bino Binazzi's[8] editorial *"In difesa dell'Accademia"* (In Defense of Academism"). It was a good indication that the magazine was on the right main road *(buona strada maestra):* "I believe that *La Brigata* will be able to serve healthy food to anyone with an appetite, operating as it will more and more as an honest inn: clean kitchen and tablecloths, and the patronage of gentlemen; without excess of waiters, service, and signs. An inn which, although patrons will come *to eat,* 'the conversations will be topical.' One must sense what is happening in the world, even if it is not spoken about. . . ."[9]

Both Rebora and Meriano were dominated by a complex and radical commitment to humanity, so clearly stated by the poet in his letter of March 5, 1917: "The world inside and outside urges me on and, like an enormous love or *mission* that cannot (yet) develop, it sickens me. . . ." The letter continues in the same vein, as he quotes from his early poem *"Clemente non fare cosí!"*

> And it is no merit, it is no sin,
> if in this matter-laden flow
> everyone, a sleeping, tossing boy,
> turns his anxious spires
> to the meaning of things.[10]

III *Womanhood*

One of Rebora's missionary activities was in praise of the dignity, inspiration, and accomplishments of women. His association with Adelaide Coari of Milan and Bice Rusconi of Florence was of prime importance toward the development of his interest in the role of women in society.

In 1926, wishing to comfort Countess Bice Rusconi who, though having marital difficulties, was meeting weekly with young women to prepare them for motherhood, Rebora wrote to her that women, using the same appeal they have to man's masculinity, should be able to attract their higher impulses and then the transformation in men will be miraculous. Women's models should be Saint Clare and Dante's Beatrice and women of the Risorgimento. Women should leave the angelic, resigned limitations of the domestic circle and extend their inspirational activities beyond the home to the *"patria della maternità"* (homeland of motherhood): "Women must develop in themselves a sentiment of universal and immortal solidarity. . . ."[11]

Even when he was outside the Church, Rebora was aware of the noble mission Christianity assigned to woman. She had the uplifting role of ennobling man and must be distinguished from the feminists agitating for liberation and battling for undifferentiated sex. She would not be an imitator or competitor of man. Her model would be Mary and the female saints—mothers, wives, virgins.

Rebora addressed women on the great task awaiting them—the task "of bringing about the maternal law of life in all fields of human activity. Man alone no longer suffices—and he strays into the selfish maleness of existence rather than into the fraternizing manliness of true progress, which is gradual realization of the divine. . . . I think all my life up to now is one of preparing myself, of becoming worthy of working in that direction, of *speaking* to woman that she may answer the call of the new age. . . . And I owe all of that to the prophetic Italian tradition, which from Clare and Beatrice, (to Maria Mazzini) had offered me shining examples and hints of woman's future mission; and in Francis, Dante, Mazzini, and Garibaldi I have found the *way* in which man helps woman to find and fulfill her miraculous life work."[12]

IV *Missionary*

Although Rebora was stricken, on December 16, 1952, with the sickness that led to his death, he joyfully continued his missionary work by answering all who wrote to him. A young seminarian requested his opinion of his own early poetry and the use he now made of poetry. His answer of November 24, 1953, is the embryo of verses and themes he used in poems that would follow: *"Il gran grido," "Poesia e santità." "Gesù il Fedele,"* and others.

Rebora began by saying it was difficult to answer his questions, that he would have to rethink the drama of his youth in its anti-Christian atmosphere, when he did not realize he was writing poetry which actually kept him from ruining himself irreparably: "Because of the reverence and the debt I owe young souls (and priestly ones!) who generously seek truth in order to give themselves totally—and full of joy to the Creator, I shall tell you something in answer to your question 'What's your opinion of Poetry?' Well: let it not be a diversion and much less an escape from sanctity, but a badge and a yearning through superabundance of Christ. . . . With regard to the *use I now make of poetry,* it seems to me that when the interior life feels the need to overflow, it fills with water little torrents which usually have no water; and it is of joy to me. . . ."[13]

With his letter, Rebora enclosed the poem *"Pesce, come fuor d'acqua boccheggi!"* (Fish, how you gasp when out of water!"), which contemplates eternal truths and recalls the words of John Stuart Mill, who wrote: "Religion and poetry address themselves, at least in one of their aspects, to the same part of the human constitution: they both supply the same want, that of ideal conceptions grander and more beautiful than we see realized in the prose of life."[14] In this letter Rebora reiterates his belief in the profound truth of the relationship between religion and poetry, both concerned with the wanderings of the soul.

Rebora's correspondence has value not only for what it reveals of his existential[15] and spiritual life but also for the originality of its language and style. It contains in embryo much of Rebora's early poetry. It is in his correspondence that he outlines his intensely lived life, his stirring emotions, his quest and findings, his formal and informal education, his struggle for recognition as both teacher and poet, his ambitions, his love of music, nature, and humanity. Often his interior conflicts reveal themselves in outbursts, by jolts, leaps, and bounds, with no apparent logic. Then one immediately feels the vehemence of his efforts to express the inexpressible. What is sometimes obscure in his poetry is clear in his correspondence, and vice versa. As Rebora's brother Piero commented to Prezzolini, "I think that some of Clemente's most beautiful writings are to be sought in his letters, some of them extraordinary."[16]

It is interesting to note that Rebora himself wrote to his friend Boine: "Idle letterwriting is for me at times a sort of lyric. . . . That's why there are days when I send six or seven, and some of them without return addresses. I can be myself with very few people and since everything is life for me—this pen, that darkness out there, my stomach making noises, and so on—I don't know what *literary falsification* means."[17] And to his friend Monteverdi: "To you who have probed me, and know me, I need not say anything else; we are two spirits who feel more than they express, who divine more than they define, and all proceeds in us through mysterious understandings."[18]

CHAPTER 19

Critics

REBORA IS CLOSER TO THIS GENERATION THAN HE WAS TO HIS OWN. Throughout his works he manifests his affinity to modern man. When his first lyric fragments appeared in 1913, the critics were not very complimentary. They may be divided into four groups: The Early Critics (1913 - 1922); The Silence (1923 - 1946), The Re-evaluation (1947 - 1960); The Recent Critics (1961 - 1977).

I *Early Critics*

Vincenzo Bucci in the *Corriere della Sera*[1] acknowledges certain uncommon lyrical qualities in Rebora's *Frammenti lirici,* and finds an echo of the philosophical poetry of Guido Guinizelli.[2] In the Socialist newspaper *Avanti!*[3] Eucardio Momigliano calls the work "an ugly book which presents a good poet." Louis Chadourne in *France-Italie* (November 1913) considers Rebora an Idealist while Emilio Cecchi calls his philosophical tendency "dangerous."

Rebora was not pleased with the reviews of the first critics nor was his publisher, Giuseppe Prezzolini, any more satisfied than he, but for other reasons. Prezzolini had labeled the new *La Voce,* directed by Giuseppe De Robertis, as a *"rivista di idealismo militante."* Not without some resentment at being used by Prezzolini as a pretext to get back at his antagonists, Rebora wrote to him: "I always found myself on this side, in the middle, beyond every *Futurism,* beyond every militancy, whether ideal or not; and I realized myself as I should have, arid in my abundance and without rest in my 'Ugolino' tower [*torre ugolinea*], which was both everybody's and nobody's piazza. I lived entirely on my own skin [*sulla mia pelle*]; and if it is typical of an ass to have harness sores, well, I accept being very much of an ass. And up to now, I have had the *cowardice* to continue not to live. But to have confused me with I know whom, is showing a lack of good taste (let alone: scruples. . . . !)"[4]

In general, the critics did not welcome his departure from traditional forms and language. Perhaps, only the reviews of two friends, which appeared the following year, were favorable. Angelo Monteverdi in *La Voce*[5] reviews Rebora's affinity to modern man, whose palpitations, anxieties, sorrows, and hopes are accented, and states that the only solution is to follow Rebora and "go among men, work hard with them, fulfill a daily concrete duty." While others remarked that Rebora's writings were full of crudities and obscurities, Monteverdi saluted him as "a poet."

The most important and fundamental review was by Giovanni Boine in *Riviera Ligure* in which he says that one "finds something Italian, that is traditionally, manfully, entirely Italian, as Italian as the lyric poetry of Dante, Michelangelo, Campanella and Bruno (as Italian as Leopardi's). . . . However, I note here [we for our part note his fondness of the repetitive manner of Charles Péguy], I still long to note here, that for much of this poetry ignored during the past year . . . deeply moved, I long to note here the word *Great."*[6]

Rebora had more than one reason to be grieved by the death of Giovanni Boine: he had been a friend since university days, and had been "the only critic who—leaving the praises aside, perhaps excessive—understood and wrote about my *Fragments,* [probing] beyond the printed lines." He did not know how many, "like me, could *live him,*" even though right then he could not *"write him."*[7] To another friend, who had also been Boine's, he wrote years later, "he is still, creatively, in my heart."[8]

Rebora and Boine had much in common regarding moral exigencies and human commitment *(l'esigenza morale e l'impegno umano).* At the Accademia Scientifico Letteraria in Milan they were both students of Gioacchino Volpe, who later recalled that they were restless spirits: "The image of Boine brought to mind Rebora—the former inclined toward philosophy, the latter toward poetry."[9]

When G. B. Parodi, another common friend of the two, learned about Rebora's conversion, he wrote an interesting letter to Adelaide Coari in which he recalled a meeting with several friends one evening in 1914. In the presence of Benedetto Croce, Rebora and Boine spoke of many things—their restlessness and intimate tragedies, their hopes and faith in the future. Croce looked at Rebora and, with much thought, slowly remarked: "You, Rebora, are the only one who works with earnestness."[10]

While Rebora's poetry was included in both Italian and French anthologies: *Poeti d'oggi*[11] and *Anthologie des poètes italiens contemporains,*[12] soon after he was forgotten.

II The Silence

During the period between 1923 - 1946, Rebora was also ignored by the major critics: DeRobertis, Falqui, Attilio Momigliano, Alfredo Gargiulo, Vittorio Rossi, Alfredo Galletti, and many others. Only Prezzolini mentions him in *La cultura italiana*[13], and Emanuel Carnevali in his book *Tales of a Hurried Man,*[14] when speaking of Italian poetry between 1910 - 1915. He was represented by eight poems in Olindo Giacobbe's anthology, *Le più belle pagine dei poeti d'oggi.*[15]

But in 1937, the silence was suddenly broken by Carlo Betocchi in *Frontespizio*. Many critics followed: Gianfranco Contini, Giuseppe Camposampiero, Carlo Bo, Giacinto Spagnoletti, and others. But to Betocchi goes the credit for having opened the path for Rebora's reevaluation, which gained momentum in 1947 when Vallecchi published *Le Poesie*—a complete edition of Rebora's poetry edited by his brother Piero. Remarkably, it stimulated renewed interest among the critics. During this period, at least twelve anthologies were added to the three already mentioned. The number of Rebora's poems included ranged from one to twelve poems, the most popular being *"Campana di Lombardia"* and *"Dall'Imagine tesa."* After 1960, the anthologies rarely failed to include Rebora. He was given his rightful place. In fact, his poetry began to appear in translation in Holland, Hungary, Jugoslavia, Russia, France, and the United States.

III Re-evaluation

Carlo Betocchi's evaluation was still the most valid. When he received a copy of *Canti dell'infermità,* he wrote to Rebora: "These verses are among your most beautiful. I cannot express my joy and gratitude on receiving this surprise. I am blessed with having been among the first to recognize the greatness of your poetry. . . ."[16]

The year 1960 closed with the first book on the life and poetry of Clemente Rebora—*L'Imagine tesa,* by Margherita Marchione. It was hailed as a milestone in Rebora criticism and was called a "fundamental work for all scholars, present and future."[17] About the same time a group of interested friends, "Amici di Clemente Rebora," sponsored the publication of a series of *Quaderni Reboriani.*[18] The first volume, a collection of writings by Mario Apollonio, Daria Banfi Malaguzzi Valeri, Remo Bessero Belti, Carlo Bo, Piero Rebora, Diego Valeri, and Carlo Zapelloni, was published in 1960. Three more volumes followed: *Lettere familiari,* edited by Piero Rebora, 1962; *Il primo Rebora,* edited by Daria Banfi Malaguzzi, 1964; *Mania dell'Eterno,* 1968 (letters and unpublished documents).

IV Recent Critics

Thereafter other books on all phases of Rebora's life and poetry followed: Marziano Guglielminetti's *Clemente Rebora* (Milan: Mursia, 1961) is a concise, scholarly study divided into three periods—the search for truth, the expectation of truth, truth itself; Renato Lollo's *La scelta tremenda, Santità e poesia nell'itinerario spirituale di Clemente Rebora* (Milan: I.P.L., 1967), a profound study of the relationship between Rebora's religious vocation and his poetic inspiration after his conversion; Maura del Serra's *Clemente Rebora: lo specchio e il fuoco* (Vita e Pensiero, 1976), a reexamination of Rebora's poetry, especially his last poems.

They were accompanied by studies and reviews in countless literary magazines and newspapers. Critics old and new were vying with one another to write on Rebora, his life and poetry, his contribution as a man and a poet to twentieth-century literature. One could give an endless list of names of writers and of radio and television programs that have treated of him.[19]

During 1977, the twentieth anniversary of Rebora's death, critics centered their attention on the publication of the first volume of Rebora's correspondence—*Lettere (1893 - 1930)*—that throws light on his long search for truth which ended in

1930, when, having made the rounds of all faiths, mystical and sociopolitical, he consciously embraced the Catholic faith.

Carlo Bo, in his preface to the *Lettere*—consisting of over one thousand leters—reiterates what has been the consensus among most of the more profound critics: "There are two Reboras, the first belongs to the history of this century's poetry; the second, who is outside time, enters into the anonymous and not decipherable history of spiritual life."[20]

CHAPTER 20

Conclusion

EXPERIENCE AND ART WERE CONCURRENT AND INSEPARABLE streams in the course of Rebora's life. Not only his poems but his letters provide a means to understanding his restless spirit, rarely at peace, never quite satisfied. His language is biographical, spiritual, meditative, full of doubt, polemics, revolt. In all his literary endeavors he expressed a love of brotherhood and truth which were woven into his biographical fabric.

Rebora was attracted only to a certain Italian tradition: not the pagan and aesthetic tradition of the Renaissance, but rather the metaphysical poetry of Dante and the *Dolce Stil Novo,* and the works of Bruno, Campanella, Leopardi. Like some of his contemporaries, he was against the feeble and long-winded Arcadia, against the aesthetes, against the opportunists of literature. But he never joined any group.

Rebora's poetry attempts to unite and almost equate poetry with thought, thought with poetry. He is more successful with free verse, which he handles felicitously to give utterance to his lyrical meditations, than with traditonal or closed meters, where the impetus is often shattered and lost. His prose is rapid, spontaneous, often in dialogue form, with brief, dry statements, similar to that of Jahier and others of *La Voce.*

Unique among the poets and writers of the twentieth century, Rebora made his poetry a manifestation of moral concerns and spiritual preoccupation: an examination of conscience, a confession, an autobiography of his soul. Basically, Rebora can be considered a moralist. However, if there were not the artist in him, we should have abandoned him to other fields and to other people.

In conclusion, it may be said that Clemente Rebora did not

Conclusion

belong to any literary school. His was an isolated endeavor. He stood on his own and by himself. He departed abruptly and almost completely from the literary style in vogue in the first years of the century. Perhaps he may be considered as one who is far from the literary influence of the past and from any literary connection with the present, and from any affiliation to the future.

Rebora's literary contribution is rich in sincerity and vitality. Like his life it is crossed by seemingly contrasting sentiments. There is a down-to-earth, almost rude expression, a spiritual view of the universe, a passion for action. Then again his dissatisfaction with material things and achievements breaks through. There is a sadness resulting from the heart's emptiness. For a long time, in the absence of a more definite target, he retreats to nature in an attempt to quench his thirst for contemplation.

Rebora's life and works are those of a searching, independent mind, of a lone climber, so to speak, of a pilgrim of the Absolute, of a man "burnt" by a mysterious fire. Once God was reached, the man and the poet plunged into Him and could not write but of Him or of all in Him. Thus ended the testimonial of a mystical experience marked by tears of anguish and joy as well as by cries of pain and ecstasy.

Clemente Rebora's poetry is the fruit of living—deep suffering, keen sorrow, bitter experiences—as well as illuminating love, sweet friendships, and the secret joy-torment in an endless search for the beauty, truth, and the goodness that is God.

Notes and References

Preface

1. Much of this material may be found in Italian in the books published by Edizioni di Storia e Letteratura: *L'Imagine Tesa,* Preface by Giuseppe Prezzolini, 1960, 300pp., 15 illustrations, and reprinted and updated in 1974, 410pp.; *Lettere,* Volume I (1893 - 1930), Preface by Carlo Bo, 1976, pp. xvi - 680, with 15 illustrations.

Chapter One

1. Pope Pius XII.
2. Rebora's letter to Margherita Marchione, November 20, 1956.
3. Cesare Angelini's letter to Margherita Marchione, November 1, 1957.
4. Armando Dominicis' letter to Margherita Marchione, March 14, 1958.
5. *Lettere di Clemente Rebora (1893 - 1930),* edited by Margherita Marchione, Preface by Carlo Bo, Edizioni di Storia e Letteratura, Rome, Italy, 1976, Volume I, 680 pp.
6. Giovanni Papini.

Chapter Two

1. Giosuè Carducci (1835 - 1907) was professor of literature at the University of Bologna from 1860 to 1904. He was a scholar, poet, editor, orator, critic, and patriot. He was awarded the 1906 Nobel Prize for literature. Carducci's verse is classic in design, with a deep and wide range of emotion. His works include *Rime* (1857), *Inno a Satana* [Hymn to Satan] (1865), *Decennali* (1871), *Nuove poesie* (1873), *Odi barbari* (1877, 1882, 1889), and *Rime nuove* (1889).
2. Giovanni Pascoli (1855 - 1912) succeeded Giosuè Carducci as professor of literature at Bologna in 1905. He wrote lyric verse of an idyllic type, sometimes disfigured by the introduction of technical words, dialect, and other irregularities but abounding in exquisite detail. He makes the peasant life of Italy as close to the life of flocks and bees

as it was in the days of Vergil or Theocritus. His Latin verses and seven volumes of Italian poems were published from 1891 to 1913. Much of his work has appeared in English.

3. Gabriele D'Annunzio (1863 - 1938), Italian poet, novelist, and dramatist whose poetry was filled with richness of imagery, sensuousness, skill in handling the language. Among his novels are *Il piacere* (1889), *L'innocente* (1892), *Il trionfo della morte* (1894). His life was crowded with sensation, but empty of real emotion. During World War I he fought with bravery in the air force, and in September 1919, he led an expedition against Fiume and established a rule opposed by the Italian government and a hostile Europe that lasted until January 1921. He was one of the few men whom Mussolini courted, having been an early exponent of Fascism. Among his plays are *Il fuoco* (1900), written during his love affair with Eleonora Duse, and *Francesca* (1902).

4. It was G. A. Borgese, in 1911, who gave these poets the name *crepuscolari* (Twilight Poets), and their movement became known as Crepuscolarism.

5. (1887 - 1907); *Piccolo libro inutile,* 1906.

6. (1885 -   ); *Poesie scritte col lapis,* 1910.

7. (1883 - 1916); *La via del rifugio,* 1906.

8. (1885 - 1975); *L'incendiario,* 1910.

9. Filippo Tommaso Marinetti (1876 - 1944), Italian poet, novelist, and critic who is best known as the founder (1909) of Futurism, on which he wrote and lectured, and as an advocate of Fascism; he was one of the first members of the Fascist party. He wrote in both French and Italian; among his works are *Le Roi Bombance* (1905) and *Mafarka le futurist* (1910).

10. Corrado Govoni (1884 - 1965) wrote his first poetical work, *Le fiale,* in 1903.

11. Paolo Buzzi (1874 - 1956) —member of the Futurist movement.

12. Joseph Cary, *Three Modern Italian Poets* (New York, 1969), p. 9.

13. *Poesia italiana contemporanea (1909 - 1959)* (Parma, 1964), p. 228.

14. The founder and editor of this review was Giuseppe Prezzolini (1882 -   ), who lived in the United States from 1930 to 1962. Professor Emeritus of Columbia University, he has written many books in English as well as in Italian, and is a regular contributor to several Italian newspapers and magazines.

Prezzolini's writings, whether scholarly or journalistic, are delightful because of his clear, precise, well-balanced style. He has a great variety of interests and his pen ranges from German mysticism to an erudite history of spaghetti, with biography, criticism, philosophy, scholarship, reportage, allegory, religion, and psychology filling the gap. (For complete bibliography of books, see *The Case of the Casa Italiana,*

1976, pp. 60 - 63; Claire Murray, "Prezzolini of Columbia," *I Am, The National Magazine for Italian-Americans*, July 1977, pp. 65 - 66.)

15. Giovanni Papini (1881 - 1956) was born in Florence. In 1903 with Prezzolini he founded the *Leonardo*. He contributed to *La Voce* and various other reviews and was editor of *Lacerba*. Shortly after World War I, Papini returned to his Catholic faith, a faith which gave his works a truly religious spirit. His approach was polemical and critical as he worked for the cultural and moral welfare of Italy. He is known world-wide for his books: *L'Uomo Finito* (translated as *The Failure)* and his *Life of Christ*. Among his poetical works are: *Poesia in versi* (1932) and *Pane e vino* (1921). Rebora's name appears in an anthology by Papini and Pancrazi which presents a panorama of Italian poetry between 1900 and 1920. The book, *Poeti d'oggi,* includes three of Rebora's poems: *"Notte a bandoliera," "O carro vuoto sul binario morto," "Il ritmo della campagna in città."* Among the forty-seven *vociani* are: Agnoletti, Bacchelli, Baldini, Boine, Campana, Cardarelli, Cecchi, Govoni, Jahier, G. P. Lucini, Onofri, Palazzeschi, Papini, Pea, Saba, Sbarbaro, Serra, Slataper, Soffici, Ungaretti, etc.

16. Ardengo Soffici (1879 - 1964), Florentine artist and writer.

17. Dino Campana (1885 - 1932) has had several editions of his *Canti Orfici* (Florence, 1928, 1942, 1952).

18. Arturo Onofri (1885 - 1928) was born in Rome. In 1912 he was editor of the short-lived review *Lirica*. He also contributed to *La Voce* and published many volumes of poetry and several volumes of literary criticism. Among his works are: *Liriche* (1907), *Terrestrità del sole* (1927), *Vincere il Drago!* (1928).

19. Giovanni Boine (1887 - 1917) joined his contemporaries in a revolt against Positivism. He sought to explore all human experiences, including the mystical. His position in the philosophical quarrels of the early twentieth century is clearly defined in his polemical writings *(Il Peccato e le altre opere,* edited by Giancarlo Vigorelli [Parma, 1971]) and his correspondence *(Carteggio Giovanni Boine,* edited by Margherita Marchione and S. E. Scalia: Vol. I *Boine-Prezzolini,* 1971; Vol. II *Boine-Cecchi,* 1972; Vol. III, 2 tomes, *Boine e gli amici del "Rinnovamento",* 1977; Vols. IV and V to follow). Boine was among the most prized contributors to cultural reviews, in particular, *La Voce, Anima,* and *La Riviera Ligure*. He also contributed various articles and book reviews to the *Rinnovamento* (1907 - 1909), a religious philosophical review published in Milan by young Catholic laymen, which spearheaded in Italy a reform movement within the Church, called Modernism. *Il Rinnovamento* elicited the admiration of England's most outstanding modernist, Baron Friedrich von Hügel. (See letter of May 23, 1907, in *Selected Letters 1896 - 1924* [New York, 1927], p. 140.)

20. Piero Jahier (1884 - 1966) contributed articles to *La Voce*. Among

his books are *Ragazzo* (Rome, 1919), and *Con me e con gli Alpini,* (Florence, 1919, and Turin, 1943).

21. The poetry and criticism that accompanied it were both called Hermetic, as things intended for the initiated only. In a certain sense the very term implied a condemnation, for it meant a difficult poetry, a cryptic manner of writing. It was, at the same time, also the expression of something new, of something revolutionary in line with what had already happened in France. It consisted, first of all, of the renunciation of too common and facile traditional forms and metrical rules, the melodiousness of trills of bel canto. It meant also the conquest of a way of expression that was direct, often analogical, stripped of all nonessentials, austere—a way of expression aiming to reach men's very roots, to say things in a pithy manner. Hermeticism abolished all ornamental oratory, the literary blandishment. It was an unfleshed poetry reduced to the essential: every word was a lyrical nucleus. It may be said in this regard that the word increases its power of expression the more it divests itself of conventional rhythms, noise, and external music. It follows almost naturally that because of its exaggerated concern for the essentials, and to the superposition of too many images and analogies, the hermetic language became incomprehensible or not easily comprehensible. It was a conquest often dangerous.

22. Giuseppe Ungaretti (1888 - 1970) was one of the most important poets of the Hermetic school. He was born in Alexandria, Egypt, of Italian parents. He studied in Paris at the Sorbonne and then went to Italy before the First World War. In 1936 he was a professor at the University of São Paulo, Brazil, and he returned to Italy in 1943. Radically innovative, Ungaretti is recognized as the foremost poet of the new generation. He began early to place great emphasis on the evocative power of the single word. While he has been accused of obscurity and deliberate confusion, his poetry has a lucidity and simplicity seldom matched in modern verse. His work is an ever-renewed quest and a confession that transcend the merely personal. Among his numerous poetical works are: *Il porto sepolto* (1916), *Allegria di naufragi* (1919), *Sentimento del tempo* (1933), *La terra promessa* (1950), and *Vita di un uomo* (1958).

23. Vincenzo Cardarelli (1887 - 1960) founded *La Ronda* in 1919.

24. Eugenio Montale (1896 -   ), Italian poet and critic. After serving in the First World War he became an editor, and later a chief librarian of the Gabinetto Vieusseux in Florence, retaining the post until the outbreak of the Second World War. His poetry attempts to reconcile external and internal experience and has been superficially compared to that of T. S. Eliot. Two of his volumes are *Ossi di seppia* (1925) and *Le occasioni* (1940). Translations of them have appeared in American and English literary journals, as have his critical writings. Montale received

Notes and References

the Nobel Prize for literature in 1975. He is presently literary critic for the *Corriere della Sera.*

25. Salvatore Quasimodo (1901 - 1968) was born in Syracuse, Sicily. His study of the Greek and Latin classics helped to give shape to his poetry. His first volume of poems, *Acque e terre,* was published in 1930, and many volumes followed, including *Giorno dopo giorno* (1947) and *La terra impareggiabile* (1958). In 1959 Quasimodo was awarded the Nobel Prize for literature. In 1960, *The Selected Writings of Salvatore Quasimodo* was published by Farrar, Straus and Cudahy. His early poetry was sometimes obscure, even surrealistic, but after World War II his work began to show more concern with reality.

26. Giacomo Leopardi (1798 - 1837) lived a life of suffering and frustration. He was a liberal and an agnostic, his poetry lofty in feeling, lyrical, but profoundly pessimistic. His early poems, *"Appressamento alla morte,"* and the odes, *"All'Italia," "Sopra il monumento di Dante,"* and *"Ad Angelo Mai"* were written before he was twenty. Toward the end of his short life he turned to political and social satire.

27. Francesco Petrarca (1304 - 1374), Italian poet and scholar who began a history of Rome in Latin, which he abandoned for a Latin epic, *Africa,* celebrating the Punic Wars. His Italian poems had become famous, and he was crowned (1341) with the laurel at Rome. He studied, hunted manuscripts, wrote in Latin and Italian, and finally retired to Arquà, where he died. Petrarca made Italy supreme in European literature, advanced the standing of letters, and was one of the first and greatest of all humanists. His Latin works are the epic *Africa; Metrical Epistles; On Contempt for the Worldly Life; On Solitude; Eclogues;* the *Letters,* invaluable as documents; and several other compositions. In Italian he wrote the *Trionfi* and the *Canzoniere,* which contains his lyrics inspired by Laura. As a sonnet writer, Petrarca is remarkable for exquisiteness and finish. His odes—for example, *"Italia mia"*—are more vigorous. Among the early English translators of the sonnets and songs were Chaucer, Spenser, Surrey, and Wyatt. Joseph Auslander translated the sonnets in 1931. (See *Petrarch,* by Thomas G. Bergin, Twayne's World Authors Series, 1970, 213 pp.)

28. *Dolce Stil Novo* (Sweet New Style) took hold in Florence, where flourishing conditions were causing an artistic awakening in the thirteenth century.

29. Jacopone da Todi (1230? - 1306), Italian religious poet, whose name was originally Jacopo Benedetti. After the sudden death of his wife, he renounced his career as a lawyer, gave his belongings to the poor, and after ten years of penance became a Franciscan tertiary. He wrote many poems full of ardent mysticism and is probably the author of the hymn *"Stabat Mater Dolorosa."* See Evelyn Underhill, *Jacopone da Todi, Poet and Mystic* (with selections, 1919); Helen C. White, *A Watch in the Night* (1933).

30. *Contemporary Italian Poetry,* University of California Press, 1962, pp. xii - xiii.
31. Giuseppe De Robertis, "Mistero a una voce," *Il Tempo,* Milano, January 19, 1956.

Chapter Three

1. Giuseppe Mazzini (1805 - 1872), patriot, philosopher, and founder of "La Giovane Italia," a secret society which led a vigorous campaign for Italian unity under a republican government.
2. Antonio Rosmini (1797 - 1855), philosopher and founder of the Order of the Rosmini Fathers.
3. Giuseppe Garibaldi (1807 - 1882), Italian patriot who fought for the unification of Italy.
4. Letter to parents, Milan, December 25, 1897, *Lettere,* I, 3. Rebora's father translated into Italian *L'esprit nouveau,* by Edgar Quinet. His mother published a book of poems entitled *Nozze d'oro. Enrico Rebora-Teresa Rebora Rinaldi 1875 - 1924* (Milano, 1924).
5. To his mother, Milan, September 11, 1904, *Lettere,* I, 5.
6. To Daria Malaguzzi, June 27, 1905, Milan, *Lettere,* I, 7. Daria was a colleague who greatly influenced a group of philosophy students. She interrupted her studies and left Milan after her first marriage. When she returned to Milan she married Antonio Banfi. She edited *Il Primo Rebora,* twenty-two unpublished letters (1905 - 1913), in 1964. Originally "La Paglia" was called "Quadrivio," later "Trivio," which recalled the "Quadrivium" and the "Trivium" of medieval schools. Its name had been changed to "La Paglia" (which Rebora called "the revised and corrected edition") at the suggestion of Daria, who came one day with a handful of straw and distributed it at the meeting. It was supposed to bring them good luck as they prepared for exams. Their Greek motto, "Nella Potenza" (In Power), was chosen by Rebora. Among the members besides Malaguzzi were Antonio Banfi, Lavinia Mazzucchetti, Angelo Monteverdi, Bianca Somaini, Sebastiano Giacomelli, Giuseppe Perini. Their friendship lasted a lifetime.
7. Antonio Banfi (1886 - 1957), philosopher and Communist senator of the Republic of Italy, founder of the review *Studi filosofici,* author of *La filosofia e la vita spirituale* (Milano, 1922), *I principi di una teoria della ragione* (Milano-Torino, 1926), *Scuola e società* (Roma, 1958), *Saggi sul marxismo* (Roma, 1960), *Filosofi contemporanei* (Milano, 1961), *Filosofia dell'arte* (Roma, 1962); Angelo Monteverdi (1886 - 1967), philologist and critic, president of the Accademia dei Lincei, codirector of *Studi medievali* and *Studi romanzi,* director of *Cultura neolatina,* author of *La leggenda di S. Eustachio* (Bergamo, 1909), *Il duomo di Cremona, il battistero e il Torrazzo* (Milano, 1911), *Le origini* (Milano, 1926), *Le origini e il Duecento* (Firenze, 1937), *Le*

origini della letteratura romanza (Roma, 1953), *Frammenti critici leopardiani* (Roma, 1959); Lavinia Mazzucchetti (1889 - 1966), translator, scholar, and author of *Schiller in Italia* (Milano, 1913), *La vita di Goethe seguita nell'epistolario* (Milano, 1932), *Goethe e il Cenacolo di Leonardo* (Milano, 1939), *L'Italia e la Svizzera,* in collab. with A. Lohner (Milano, 1943), *R. M. Rilke, Lettere milanesi* (Milano, 1956), *Novecento in Germania* (Milano, 1959). Translator of Th. Mann, S. Zweig, H. Carossa, J. Roth, E. Wiechert, etc.

8. To Angelo Monteverdi, Codogno, November 15, 1906, *Lettere* I, 13 - 14.
9. To Daria Malaguzzi, Milano, September 15, 1906, *Lettere* I, 11.
10. *Ibid.,* February 1, 1907, *Lettere* I, 16 - 18.
11. *Ibid.*
12. *Ibid.*
13. *Ibid.,* March 17, 1907, *Lettere* I, 18 - 19.
14. *Ibid.*
15. *Ibid.,* September 18, 1907, *Lettere* I, 22 - 23.
16. To Angelo Monteverdi, Milan, July 31, 1907, *Lettere,* I, 20 - 21.
17. *"O carro vuoto sul binario morto."*
18. A. Giarreietto, "Nella religione cattolica ho trovato la luce," *Fiori di Passione,* August 1952.
19. To Angelo Monteverdi, Milan, June 21. 1906, *Lettere,* I, 9.
20. *Ibid.,* Milan, July 27, 1906, *Lettere,* I, 10.
21. *Ibid.,* Sabbio Chise, August 8, 1906, *Lettere,* I, 10.
22. *Ibid.,* August 10, 1906, *Lettere,* I, 11.
23. *Ibid.,* August 10, 1906, *Lettere,* I, 11.
24. *Ibid.,* Codogno, November 15, 1906, *Lettere,* I, 13 - 14.
25. *Ibid.,* Milan, December 26, 1906, *Lettere,* I, 14.
26. To Daria Malaguzzi, Milan, February 8, 1909, *Lettere,* I, 40.
27. To Antonio Banfi, Milan, August 4, 1911, *Lettere,* I, 94.

Chapter Four

1. Giandomenico Romagnosi (1761 - 1835), the nineteenth-century Italian educator-philosopher, specialized in penal and criminal law.
2. *Heroici furori* by Giordano Bruno (1548 - 1600), Italian philosopher condemned and burned at the stake for heresy.
3. Giovanni Battista Vico (1668 - 1744), Italian philosopher who wrote *Scienza nuova.* His new poetic theory was not fully appreciated until the nineteenth century. His work is the first survey of the social evolution of mankind and the first to recognize the superiority of imagination over reason, as well as the unity of spirit and knowledge created by man himself. It was enthusiastically accepted by Goethe, Michelet, Foscolo, Mazzini, DeSanctis, Coleridge, Croce, Joyce, Yeats.

4. Vittorio Alfieri (1749 - 1803) wrote twenty tragedies. He was an opponent of the rationalistic century in which he was born.

5. To his father, Loveno, October 22, 1909, *Lettere,* I, 53 - 54.

6. Vol. II, pp. 808 - 40, November 15, 1911.

7. To Giuseppe Prezzolini, Milan, January 13, 1911, *Lettere,* I, 77 - 79.

8. To Lavinia Mazzucchetti, Loveno, August 21, 1912, *Lettere,* I, 130 - 31.

9. See *Political Thought: Men and Ideas,* by John A. Abbo (Westminster, Maryland, 1960), p. 216: "According to the idealists, ideas are the essential factors in knowledge: there is nothing beyond our idea and our knowledge, and it is by our intellectual activity alone that everything is explained. As an ethical doctrine, idealism struck hard at the hedonistic concept of utilitarian liberalism (life is a pursuit of self-interest, and pleasure the spring of human action). The idealists put the accent on duty, not on gratification or calculation or even right. They saw life as a tremendously exacting and heroic affair. For them, man's purpose was to achieve perfect spiritual freedom—a purpose to be realized by stages with the help of law, morality, society, and religion. As a political theory, idealism was an extreme effort to turn away from the individualistic outlook and atomism of the democratic revolution, which had limited and therefore in a sense minimized the authority and the functions of the state. The idealists (pantheists, mystics, and romantics combined) extolled the national state to unparalleled heights. They denied its creation by individuals or families or other social groups. They viewed its authority as unlimited, its law as the infallible expression of justice, its citizens as absorbed by and in it so as to become fully free."

10. *France-Italie,* November 1, 1913.

11. *La Tribuna,* November 12, 1913.

12. To Giuseppe Prezzolini, Milan, January 13, 1911, *Lettere,* I, 77 - 79.

Chapter Five

1. Letter to Daria Malaguzzi, Treviglio, November 29, 1910, *Lettere,* I, 74 - 75.

2. *Ibid.,* Milan, November 25, 1914, *Lettere,* I, 246 - 48.

3. Letter to Angelo Monteverdi, Milan, January 30, 1910, *Lettere,* I, 60 - 61.

4. Francesco Novati (1859 - 1915), philologist, professor of neo-Latin literatures, Accademia Scientifico-Letteraria, Milan.

5. Michele Scherillo (1860 - 1930), professor of Italian literature, Accademia Scientifico-Letteraria, Milan.

6. Letter to Angelo Monteverdi, Milan, January 30, 1910, *Lettere,* I, 60 - 61.
7. *Ibid.,* March 4, 1910, *Lettere,* I, 61.
8. *Ibid.,* April 16, 1910, *Lettere,* I, 63.
9. *Ibid.,* September 17, 1910, *Lettere,* I, 69.
10. *Ibid.,* September 28, 1910, *Lettere,* I, 70.
11. *Ibid.,* Treviglio, November 22, 1910, *Lettere,* I, 73 - 74.
12. Letter to Daria Malaguzzi, Milan, March 2, 1911, *Lettere,* I, 82.
13. *Ibid.,* Milan, November 16, 1911, *Lettere,* I, 104.
14. Letter to Angelo Monteverdi, Milan, June 18, 1911, *Lettere,* I, 90 - 91.
15. Letter to Daria Malaguzzi, Milan, November 16, 1911, *Lettere,* I, 106.

Chapter Six

1. Letter to Antonio Banfi, Milan, June 20, 1911, *Lettere,* I, 92.
2. *Ibid.,* September 6, 1911, *Lettere,* I, 97.
3. Letter to Daria Malaguzzi, Milan, November 16, 1911, *Lettere,* I, 105 - 106.
4. Letter to Lavinia Mazzucchetti, Milan, March 10, 1912, *Lettere,* I, 117.
5. Letter to Giuseppe Prezzolini, Milan, March 11, 1912, *Lettere,* I, 118.
6. *Ibid.,* March 26, 1912.
7. Letter to Cesarina Rossi, Milan, December 9, 1912, *Lettere,* I, 137 - 38.
8. Letter to Daria Malaguzzi, Milan, August 16, 1912, *Lettere,* I, 128 - 29.
9. Letter to Angelo Monteverdi, Loveno, August 20, 1912, *Lettere,* I, 130.
10. Letter to Daria Malaguzzi, Milan, May 19, 1911, *Lettere,* I, 89 - 90.
11. Letter to Antonio Banfi, Milan, March 5, 1912, *Lettere,* I, 116 - 117.
12. *Ibid.,* September 25, 1911, *Lettere,* I, 100 - 102.
13. Letter to Daria Malaguzzi, Milan, June 28, 1912, *Lettere,* I, 123 - 24.
14. *Ibid.,* Treviglio, May 1, 1911, *Lettere,* I, 87.

Chapter Seven

1. Cesare Angelini in his letter of December 14, 1956, wrote to Margherita Marchione: "Prezzolini, the necessary Italian to whom we

must attribute all the literary good that was accomplished during the past fifty years in Italy, and not only in this period. A born educator, Prezzolini has taught and continues to teach, a man who augments in giving: giving ideas, counsel, orientation, mind and heart. With *La Voce* he has created the palaestra to which the living and the dead who still count in Italy have given the measure of their genius and their artistic ability."

2. Papini, *Un uomo finito* (Florence, 1912); Slataper, *Il mio Carso* (Florence, 1912); Serra, *Esame di coscienza d'un letterato* (Milano, 1916); Jahier, *Ragazzo* (Roma, 1919); Soffici, *Lemmonio Boreo* (Florence, 1912); Sbarbaro, *Trucioli* (Florence, 1920); Rebora, *Frammenti lirici* (Florence, 1913).

3. Letter to Angelo Monteverdi, June 18, 1911, Milan. *Lettere*, I, 90 - 91.

4. *Il Rinnovamento*, a weekly magazine (1907 - 1909), edited by A. A. Alfieri, A. Casati, and T. Gallarati Scotti, was condemned for its modernist ideas by the ecclesiastic authorities. Among the collaborators were S. Jacini, G. Boine. Cfr. *Giovanni Boine—Amici del 'Rinnovamento'* (Roma, 1977).

5. Giovanni Amendola (1882 - 1926), political leader, collaborator of *Leonardo* and then of *La Voce*.

6. *La Voce*, February 27, 1913.

7. *Ibid.*, March 28, 1914.

8. Mondadori, Milan, 1923, pp. 181 - 87.

9. *La Voce*, May 8, 1913.

10. *Ibid.*, July 31, 1913.

11. A. Giarreietto, "Nella religione cattolica ho trovato la luce," in *Fiori di passione*, August 1952.

12. Letter to G. Boine, July 16, 1914, Milan, I, 223 - 24.

13. Letter to A. Monteverdi, January 14, 1912, Milan, I, 110.

14. Letter of Piero Rebora, July 17, 1957, to Margherita Marchione.

15. Carlo Bo, "Rebora, Il poeta che tacque per diventare umile frate," *La Stampa*, Turin, November 2, 1957.

16. November 2, 1952.

Chapter Eight

1. *The Literary Works of Leonardo da Vinci, (Scritti letterari di Leonardo da Vinci)* ed. Jean Paul Richter and Irma A. Richter (London, 1939), II, 324.

2. Letter to Daria Malaguzzi, Milan, Feb. 12, 1912, *Lettere*, I, 113 - 14.

3. Letter to Antonio Banfi, Milan, Feb. 12, 1912, *Lettere*, I, 112 - 13.

4. The reference is to *"Inno a Satana"* by Giosuè Carducci.

Chapter Nine

1. Letter of Marino Moretti to Prezzolini, May 10, 1958. The poem was published in *La Grande Illustrazione,* July 1914.
2. Letter to Piero Rebora, Milan, June 27, 1914, *Lettere,* I, 220.
3. Letter to Giuseppe Prezzolini, Milan, September 22, 1913, *Lettere,* I, 193.
4. Letter to Giovanni Boine, Milan, July 16, 1914, *Lettere,* I, 223 - 224.
5. Letter to Piero Rebora, Milan, June 27, 1914, *Lettere,* I, 220 - 221.
6. Letter to Angelo Monteverdi, Milan, July 16, 1914, *Lettere,* I, 224.
7. Letter to Antonio Banfi, Milan, August 1, 1914, *Lettere,* I, 223.

Chapter Ten

1. Of her ability, Ada Negri, twentieth-century Italian poet, wrote (See *Music Program,* March 23, 1930): "If I knew how to play the piano, I would like to play like Lydia Natus, who can say with her heart on the tips of her fingers how much she can suffer, how much she can love."
2. Letter to Giovanni Boine, Milan, December 8, 1914, *Lettere,* I, 248.
3. Letter of Lydia Natus to Giovanni Boine, Milan, December 3, 1914. See Margherita Marchione, *Nuova Antologia,* "L'altro amore di Clemente Rebora," June 1970, pp. 220 - 21.
4. Letter to Margherita Marchione, August 12, 1959.
5. Letter to Sibilla Aleramo, Oct. 11, 1914, Milan, *Lettere,* I, 240 - 41. Rina Faccio—whose pseudonym was Sibilla Aleramo—one of the more important novelists of contemporary Italian literature, was born in 1875 and died in 1960. In 1906 she wrote an autobiographical novel, *Una donna,* which was translated into English *(A Woman at Bay)* and published by G. P. Putnam, London, in 1908. It was considered a feminist document. In 1932 she wrote her fourth novel, *Il frustino.* In it she describes her love for Clemente Rebora, giving him the fictitious name Emanuele. (See article by Margherita Marchione, *"L'altro amore di Clemente Rebora,"* in Nuova Antologia, June 1970.)
6. "Fragment XXX."
7. Leonid Andreyev, *Lazzaro e altre novelle* (Florence, 1919); Nikolai Gogol, *Il Cappotto* (versione, nota, annotazioni di Clemente Rebora) (Milan, 1922); Leo Tolstoi, *La felicità domestica,* (Florence, 1920; 2nd edition, Milan, 1942).
8. Leonid Nikolaevich Andreyev (1871 - 1919), Russian short-story writer and playwright, became the spokesman for the intellectuals in the twilight era around 1900.

9. Taddei, Ferrara, 1921. See also "Letteratura straniera in Italia," *Energie Nove,* September 30, 1919, pp. 166 - 68.

10. Francesco Meriano was editor and founder, with Bino Binazzi, of *La Brigata.* Perhaps the title of this review was inspired by Rebora, who wrote a couplet that appears on the first two issues: *"Noi siam dell'inquieta brigata/ e scontentezza ci guida"* (We belong to the restless group/ and are led by discontent).

11. *L'Ardita,* 1919, pp. 309 - 10.

12. Leo Nikolaevich Tolstoi (1828 - 1910), Russian novelist and philosopher, one of the world's great writers.

13. Letter to Francesco Meriano, Milan, July 17, 1919, *Lettere,* I, 377.

14. Regarding this manuscript, see Lydia Natus's letter to Francesco Meriano, *Lettere,* I, 322.

15. Fedor Mikhailovich Dostoevski (1821 - 1881), famous Russian novelist.

16. Letter to Prezzolini, Milan, July 24, 1919, *Lettere,* I, 378 - 79.

17. Letter to his mother, Milan, July 17, 1919, *Lettere,* I, 376 - 77.

18. Nikolai Vasilevich Gogol (1809 - 1852), Russian short-story writer, novelist, and playwright. He was the herald of Realism in Russian literature.

19. Letter to Sibilla Aleramo, Milan, September 14, 1922, including text of her letter to Rebora, *Lettere,* I, 436 - 37.

20. The following poem, written by Gogol and translated by Clemente Rebora, appeared in *Russia,* a review of literary art and history edited by Ettore Lo Gatto (Rome, 1920 - 21), pp. 209 - 10. Rebora accompanied his translation of Gogol's poem "Italia" with a commentary explaining that it had been inserted in his complete works of the Edizione di Pietroburgo, 1900, vol. IX, pp. 49 - 50. He explains how he tried to interpret the meaning of the Russian text as well as the sound. Gogol imagined Italy as "the symbol of a generous sensuality that could purify itself in beauty, the revealer of a true poetical religion. . . ."

"Italia"

Italia—magnificente paese!
Per te l'anima geme, e si strugge:
Tu sei paradiso, tu piena letizia,
E in te smagliante amor ha primavera.
Fantasticando l'onda fugge, fiotta
E prodigiose rive bacia;
Rilucon bellissimi i cieli,
Avvampa il limone, e spira l'aroma.

Da ogni parte ti avvolge l'afflato,
Dovunque l'impronta dei tempi riposa.

> E il viaggiatore si affretta
> Da plaghe nevose, già ardendo,
> E il grande creato contempla:
> L'anima ferve; intenerir si sente,
> Trema negli occhi una lagrima inconscia:
> Assorto nel cuor sognatore
> Attinge l'eco di remote cose.
>
> Del mondo qui la fredda vanità inabissa,
> Non si snatura l'orgoglioso ingegno;
> In iridato nimbo di bellezza
> Più terso e acceso il sol va per lo spazio.
> Mirabili visioni, mirabili clangori
> Qui il mare in pace all'improvviso effonde;
> Trànsito vivo di nubi lo svaria,
> Il verde bosco, e la celeste volta.
>
> Ma notte, notte, in estasi respiri:
> Come dorme la terra, inebriata e adorna!
> Appassionato il mirto la sfiora;
> E tu, alta sul mondo, luna
> Fulgida guardi, e meditando ascolti
> Come gorgogli l'acqua sotto il remo,
> Come su dalle aiole si espanda un concento,
> Che incantevole lungi risuona e fluisce.
>
> Terra d'amore e mare di magìe!
> Nel mondial deserto giardino di luce!
> Giardino dove tra il vapor dei sogni
> Vivon Torquato e Raffaello ancora!
> Ti vedro io, trepido d'attesa?
> Radioso il cuore, sgorganti i pensieri,
> Mi brucia e seduce il tuo soffio:
> Io nel ciel tutto pàlpito e suono!

21. Margherita Marchione, "La storia d'amore di Clemente Rebora," *Le Fiera Letteraria*, Rome, September 27, 1959.

Chapter Eleven

1. Dal *Diario Sentimentale dal luglio 1914 al maggio 1915* di A. Panzini (Milan, 1923), pp. 181 - 87.
2. Letter to Sibilla Aleramo, April 2, 1915, *Lettere,* I, 254 - 55.
3. Letter to Giuseppe Prezzolini, April 3, 1915, *Lettere,* I, 255.
4. Letter to his mother, April 17, 1915, *Lettere,* I, 256.
5. *Ibid.,* April 25, 1915, *Lettere,* I, 257 - 58.
6. *Ibid.,* May 6, 1915, *Lettere,* I, 259 - 60.
7. *Ibid.,* August 24, 1915, *Lettere,* I, 265.

8. Dal *Diario Sentimentale dal luglio 1914 al maggio 1915* di A. Panzini (Milan, 1923), pp. 181 - 87.
9. Letter to Sibilla Aleramo, August 5, 1914, *Letter,* I, 234.
10. Letter to Daria Malaguzzi, August 28, 1914, *Lettere,* I, 235.
11. Letter to Michele Cascella, September 18, 1914, *Lettere,* I, 238.
12. Letter to his father, November 10, 1915, *Lettere,* I, 273 - 74.
13. Letter to his mother, November 28 - 29, 1915, *Lettere,* I, 275.
14. *Ibid.,* December 1, 1915, *Lettere,* I, 276.
15. Letter to Lavinia Mazzucchetti, December 3, 1915, *Lettere,* I, 276 - 77.
16. Letter to his mother, December 8, 1915, *Lettere,* I, 279.
17. *Dal letto della sua infermità: 1955.*
18. Letter of Giuseppe Martorano to Margherita Marchione, August 9, 1957.
19. Letter to Giuseppe Martorano, July 17, 1916, *Lettere,* I, 293.
20. See article by Margherita Marchione, "Clemente Rebora nel panorama letterario," *Rassegna di politica e di storia,* April 1969, 106 - 107. "God made us see Italy." *La Lettura,* Milan, December 1, 1916.
21. "Home guardsman counseled." *La Brigata,* Bologna, December 1916.
22. "Think it over again" and "Rear-line whimsy and chorale." *Riviera Ligure,* Oneglia, January 1, 1917.
23. "Calendar" and "Bell-ringing with angels." *La Brigata,* Bologna, January 1917.
24. "Without fanfare." *La Diana,* Naples, March 1917.
25. "Pruning" and "Forgiveness?" *La Brigata,* Bologna, April 1917.
26. "Right on time" and "Close-mouthed chorus." *Riviera Ligure,* Oneglia, May 1, 1917.
27. "Rainbows over the gore." *La Brigata,* Bologna, May 1917.
28. "Fountain in the rubble." *La Raccolta,* Bologna, July 15, 1918.
29. Letter to Colonel Giovanni Capristo, Milan, November 3, 1925. *Lettere,* I, 488 - 90.
30. *La Raccolta,* Bologna, May 15, 1918.
31. *Ibid.*
32. *La Raccolta,* Bologna, July 15, 1918.
33. *Ibid.*

Chapter Twelve

1. Blaise Pascal (1623 - 1662), French scientist and philosopher.
2. *Le Mystère de Jésus:* ". . . tu ne chercherais pas, si tu ne m'avais trouvé," (cfr. Pascal's *Pensées*).

Notes and References

3. Carlo Betocchi, "La Poesia di Clemente Rebora," *L'Albero,* January 1950.
4. Giacinto Spagnoletti, "Un poeta convertito," *La Fiera Letteraria,* October 10, 1948.
5. Ferruccio Ulivi, *Antologia della Poesia Religiosa* (Florence, 1952), p. 110.

Chapter Thirteen

1. Giuseppe Mazzini (1805 - 1872), Italian patriot, political theorist, and critic, was born and raised in Genoa. He attended the Royal College, where lectures on the classics extolled the virtues of republics and of ancient Rome. He was graduated from the university in 1827, a Doctor of Law. He formed a brotherhood to smuggle contraband books. In 1830 he joined the Carbonari Society, once an Italian revolutionary movement, but he soon lost belief in its aimless ritualism. While in prison he formulated his life's program: "Italy One and Independent, with Rome for Capital." He chose exile and organized, agitated, conspired, spoke and wrote to unite Italy. Believing that the future lay in the hands of youth, he formed *Giovane Italia* (Young Italy). From France he went to Switzerland. The moderates began to consider union under the Piedmont monarchy. Mazzini was opposed. He returned to Italy to join the 1848 and 1849 revolts that did not succeed. In 1872, he died in Pisa. A National Edition of Mazzini's works, begun in 1906, has now reached 100 volumes, and is not yet complete.
2. Letter to his mother, August 5, 1912, *Lettere,* I, 127 - 28.
3. Letter to Daria Malaguzzi, September 4, 1912, *Lettere,* I, 133.
4. Letter to Antonio Banfi, December 10, 1912, *Lettere,* I, 138 - 39.
5. *"Nella seral turchina oscurità."*
6. Letter to his brother Piero, November 18, 1922, *Lettere,* I, 441.
7. *The Life of Mazzini,* by Bolton King, Everyman's Library (London/New York, 1911), pp. 245 - 46.
8. *Ibid.,* pp. 256 - 57.
9. *Ibid.,* pp. 263 - 64.
10. *Giuseppe Mazzini: Selected Writings,* edited by N. Gangulee (London, 1945), p. 139.

Chapter Fourteen

1. Letter of E. Levi to Margherita Marchione, August 26, 1957.
2. Duke Tommaso Gallarati Scotti (1878 - 1966), author and diplomat. Born in Milan of an ancient and noble family, he was influenced by Antonio Fogazzaro (1842 - 1911), novelist and representa-

tive of Modernist Catholic thought in Italian literature, and Friedrich von Hügel (1852 - 1925), Roman Catholic theologian, founder of the London Society for the Study of Religion. He participated actively in the Modernist Movement until it was condemned, and was one of the founders of *Il Rinnovamento*. Among his literary works are: *The Life of Antonio Fogazzaro; The Life of Dante*.

3. Letter to his brother Piero, Milan, April 18, 1921, *Lettere*, I, 410 - 11.

4. Rabindranath Tagore (1861 - 1941), Indian poet, dramatist, and novelist. He received the Nobel Prize for literature in 1913. Born in Calcutta, he was educated both in India and in England. He published novels, plays, short stories, and poetry.

5. Letter to Rabindranath Tagore, September 18, 1921, Milan, *Lettere*, I, 419 - 20.

6. "The Aldwych Series," consisted of dainty reprints of old, rare, thin volumes, none of which exceeded 250 copies.

7. Janârdana, pp. 58 - 59.

8. *Ibid.*, pp. 63 - 64.

9. Preface to *Libretti di Vita*.

10. The series was to have 60 volumes, but it failed after the sixteenth: Guyau G. M., *La fede dell'avvenire,* a cura del prof. A. Banfi, 1924. Böhme, Jacob, *Scritti di religone,* a cura del prof. A. Banfi, 1924. *Il Talmud.* Scelta di massime, parabole, leggende, a cura dei proff. Beilinson e D. Lattes, 1924. *Regola di Santo Benedetto,* a cura del prof. A. Hermet, 1924. Lambruschini R., *Armonie della vita umana,* a cura del prof. A. Linacher, 1925. *Scritti religiosi dei riformatori italiani del 1500,* a cura del dott. Piero Chiminelli, 1925. *Scritti per la conferenza mondiale delle chiese cristiane,* a cura del prof. A. Palmieri, 1925. Solovjòv V., *Il bene nella natura umana,* a cura del prof. E. Lo Gatto, 1925. Towianski, *Lo spirito e l'azione,* a cura della prof. Maria Bersano Begey, 1925. *Ammaestramenti morali* di Fra Jacopone, a cura del prof. Piero Rebora, 1925. Cantideva, *In cammino verso la luce,* a cura del prof. G. Tucci, 1925. Plotino, *Dio.* Scelta e traduzione dalle "Enneadi," con introduzione di A. Banfi, 1925. Gioberti V., *L'Italia, la Chiesa e la Civiltà universale.* Pagine scelte a cura di A. Bruers, 1926. *La verità ti libererà.* Pagine scelte dall'*Imitazione di Cristo,* a cura di Giovanni Semprini, 1926. *Le regole e il testamento* di San Francesco, a cura di Augusto Hermet, 1926. *Saggezza cinese.* Scelta di massime, parabole e leggende, a cura del prof. G. Tucci, 1926.

11. Letter to Adelaide Coari, Milan, November 17, 1924, *Lettere*, I, 474 - 75. She was a well-known educator of the "Gruppo d'Azione delle scuole del popolo," who helped Rebora during the period of his conversion and after.

Notes and References

12. Letter to Piero Rebora, Milan, October 27, 1922, *Lettere,* I, 437 - 40.

13. Italian Fascism was a political movement, not the result of ideological preparation but of certain historical conditions, namely: the formation of a class of unemployed veterans; the personal magnetism of Mussolini (1883 - 1945), its founder and leader; the devaluation of the *lira* following the World War I; the decline of the Italian parliamentary system; the split in the Socialist party following the rise of Russian Communism.

14. Letter of Piero Rebora to Margherita Marchione, August 6, 1957.

15. "A group of [University and Secondary School] professors and [Primary School] teachers, conscious of the responsibility of their task as educators, feel duty bound to publicly voice their painful and shocked amazement vis-a-vis the indifference and inaction of the Minister of Public Education on the occasion of the murder of the Hon. Matteotti, a crime undermining the very foundation of the moral structure of the State, theoretically claimed as the ideal objective of the Hon. Gentile's philosophic doctrine. They further declare that they do not feel they are being represented by a philosopher minister who, after what happened, still continues to head the Italian school system. (See A. Banfi, *Umanità*. Autobiographical pages arranged by Daria Banfi Malaguzzi. Preface by Michele Ranchetti. Edizioni Franco, Reggio Emilia, 1967, 203 - 204.)

16. Letter to his brother Piero, Milan, January 6, 1926, *Lettere,* I, 496. On his letterhead, Rebora used the following: *"L'Italia dell'Umanità. Meritate e avrete* (Mazzini). *L'unione e l'amore rivelano ai popoli le vie del Signore* (Mamèli)" [The Italy of Humanity. Be deserving and you will have (Mazzini). Union and love reveal to peoples the way of the Lord (Mamèli)].

17. Letter to Giovanni Capristo, Milan, November 3, 1925, *Lettere,* I, 489.

Chapter Fifteen

1. See Piero Rebora's article "Clemente Rebora e la sua prima formazione esistenzialista," *Humanitas,* pp. 114 - 25.

2. Letter to his brother Piero, Milan, January 6, 1926, *Lettere,* I, 495 - 97.

3. Letter of Piero Rebora to Giuseppe Prezzolini, Milan, September 5, 1956, made available to the author by recipient.

4. Scillitan Martyrs, from the place of their martyrdom in Africa, Scillium, in 180 A.D.

5. Letter to his brother Piero, Milan, May 25, 1928, *Lettere,* I, 576 - 78.

6. *Ibid.*, November 11, 1928, *Lettere,* I, 587.
7. Letter of September 2, 1936, to Cardinal Schuster in *Charitas,* November 1977, p. 335.
8. As an infant, Rebora had been baptized a Roman Catholic in the church of S. Francesca Romana, but was not raised in the faith.
9. In the historical novel by Alessandro Manzoni, *I Promessi Sposi,* Lucia represents the simple, uncomplicated faith of the honest poor and the spirit of Christian charity and humility in action. Her candor, innocence, and unquestioning faith provoke a spiritual crisis in the Innominato, a social rebel who is thereby turned into a great force for good.

Chapter Sixteen

1. See Margherita Marchione, "Linguaggio reboriano," *Lingua Nostra,* Florence, September 1959.
2. This poem was first published in the 1947 edition of *Le Poesie.*

Chapter Seventeen

1. From the Minutes of the "Cittadella" Award, 1956.
2. Council of Trent, 1545 - 1563.
3. Margherita Marchione visited Rebora during the summer of 1957.
4. Letter to his brother Piero, June 22, 1946, Archivio Rosminiano.
5. Silvio Pellico (1788 - 1854), patriot-martyr, author of *Le mie prigioni.*
6. *"Pesce, come fuor d'acqua boccheggi,"* written in March 1953. (See p. 180.)
7. Letter to his brother Piero, June 6, 1946, Archivio Rosminiano.
8. *Le Poesie,* Vallecchi, Florence, 1947 [*Frammenti lirici* (1903 - 1913), *Poesie varie* (1913 - 1918), *Canti anonimi* (1920 - 1922), and several unpublished poems written between 1934 and 1947].
9. Letter to Mario Costanzo, October 6, 1954, Archivio Rosminiano.
10. Letter to his brother Piero, August 14, 1951, Archivio Rosminiano.
11. *Ibid.,* November 12, 1950, Archivio Rosminiano.
12. Arthur Rimbaud (1854 - 1891), French poet, a precursor of Symbolism.
13. Ezra Loomis Pound (1885 - 1972), American poet and critic who lived in Italy, and in January 1941 began broadcasting Fascist propaganda by shortwave from Rome to the United States.

Chapter Eighteen

1. Letter to Antonio Banfi, Milan, January 23, 1913, *Lettere,* I, 144 - 45.
2. Bruno Furlotti (1894 - 1970), artist and friend from Verona.
3. Francesco Meriano (1896 - 1934), editor of *La Brigata,* diplomat and author of *Equatore notturno,* Edizioni futuriste di poesia, 1916 and *Croci di legni,* Vallecchi, 1919.
4. Countess Jahn Rusconi.
5. Letter to Bruno Furlotti, Milan, September 28, 1920, *Lettere,* I, 399 - 401.
6. Rainer Maria Rilke (1875 - 1926), German poet.
7. *Letters to a Young Poet,* translated by M. D. Herter (New York, 1954).
8. Associate editor of *La Brigata.* See February-March 1917 issue, pp. 145 - 49: ". . . But let's try to draw a somewhat practical conclusion from our "academic" chit-chat. While we greatly respect Marinetti and the first initiators and promoters of Futurism . . . we proclaim here and now our definitive return to tradition, to the difficulties inherent in forms, in complicated meters, in aristocratic idiom—in all that constitutes an effective obstacle against the panhandlers of intelligence and against loafers and freebooters. True poets, if there be any among us, will not only survive, but grow stronger in our palestra. The others will not have wasted their time, for though their works will go into the void, they themselves will have acquired a precious gift: the full knowledge of our great literature, a knowledge which will make them more conscious of the nobility of our people, and more sincerely devoted to Italy. Which is what will make of them something more decent than a puny dolt, a fraud both as poet and as prose writer, and as 'freeworded' as he is liberally ignorant and presumptuous."
9. Letter to Francesco Meriano, Milan, March 1, 1917, *Lettere,* I, 315 - 17.
10. *Ibid.,* March 5, 1917, 317 - 18.
11. Letter to Bice Rusconi, Milan, July 1, 1926, *Lettere,* I, 501 - 502.
12. *Ibid.,* August 11, 1926, 507.
13. Letter to Giovanni Salzotti, Stresa, November 24, 1953. See *L'Imagine tesa,* 1974, 329 - 30.
14. John Stuart Mill, *Essays on Religion,* Chapter III.
15. With regard to his existential ideas, Clemente Rebora believed in the individual's responsibility for making himself what he is.
16. Letter of Piero Rebora to Giuseppe Prezzolini, September 2, 1956.
17. Letter to Giovanni Boine, Milan, July 29, 1914, *Lettere,* I, 230.

18. Letter to Angelo Monteverdi, Milan, October 5, 1905, *Lettere,* I, 24.

Chapter Nineteen

1. July 16, 1913.
2. Guido Guinizelli. See note on *Dolce Stil Novo,* p. 200.
3. September 16, 1913.
4. Letter to Giuseppe Prezzolini, Milan, January 15, 1914, *Lettere,* I, 205.
5. April 13, 1914.
6. September 1914.
7. Letter to Francesco Meriano, Villa Serafina, May 26, 1917, *Lettere,* I, 327.
8. Letter to Adelaide Coari, Milan, May 18, 1919, *Lettere,* I, 373.
9. Letter of Gioacchino Volpe to Carlo Martini, February 19, 1960.
10. Letter of G. B. Parodi to Adelaide Coari, December 24, 1929. It is interesting to note that even Boine's mother recognized Rebora's "earnestness," asking him to edit all her son's philosophical writings (see letter of July 5, 1918, to his mother, *Lettere,* I, 354).
11. Papini-Pancrazi, *Poeti d'oggi* (Antologia 1900 - 1920). Florence, 1920, 1925. Here one also finds biographical and bibliographical references sent by Rebora to Pancrazi (see letter to Pietro Pancrazi, April 8, 1919, *Lettere,* I, 371 - 72).
12. Jean Chuzeville, *Anthologie des poètes italiens contemporains* (1880 - 1920). Paris, 1921. The "introduction" is written by Maurice Mignon.
13. *La Voce,* Florence, 1923, 1930, 1938.
14. Contact Editions, Paris, 1925. "And then Clemente Rebora, very earnest and very rich, who overflows into an imagism that is an orgy of cold senses, and dwindles into a unanimism that is emotional vagueness."
15. Vol. IV, Carabba, 1928.
16. Letter of Carlo Betocchi to Clemente Rebora, October 23, 1956. (See *L'Imagine tesa,* p. 213.)
17. *Civiltà Cattolica,* November 11, 1961.
18. All'insegna del Pesce d'Oro, Milan, 1960.
19. Luciano Anceschi, G. B. Angioletti, Riccardo Bacchelli, Giorgio Bàrbari Squarotti, Angelo Barile, Pasquale Bricchi, Francesco Bruno, Glauco Cambon, Giorgio Caproni, Giuseppe Cantamessa, Paolo DeBenedetti, Italo de Feo, Gherardo Del Colle, Idilio Dell'Era, Giuseppe DeSimone, Enzo Fabiani, Nazareno Fabbretti, Giovanni Fallani, Alberto Frattini, Carmelo Giovannini, Giovanni Getto, Giovanni Giudici, Giovanni Grazzini, Francesco Grisi, Mario Luzi, Oreste Macrì, Mario Marcazan, Giuseppe Marchetti, Umberto

Marvardi, Artal Mazzotti, Eugenio Montale, Alessandro Parronchi, Domenico Porzio, Giuseppe Raimondi, Giuseppe Ravignani, Clemente Riva, Vincenzo Sala, Edoardo Sanguineti, Luigi Santucci, Margherita Sarfatti, Ines Scaramucci, Adriano Seroni, Carmelina Sicari, Giovanni Titta Rosa, Claudio Toscani, Franco Trifuoggi, Angelo Ubiali, Alfeo Valle, Ezio Viola, Valerio Volpini, Giannino Zanelli.

20. *Lettere di Clemente Rebora,* Preface by Carlo Bo, v - xiii.

Selected Bibliography

PRIMARY SOURCES

"Per un Leopardi mal noto," *Rivista d'Italia,* Roma, September 1910.
"G. D. Romagnosi nel pensiero del Risorgimento," *Rivista d'Italia,* Roma, November 1911.
Frammenti lirici. Libreria della Voce, Firenze, 1913.
Canti anonimi. Il Convegno Editoriale, Milano, 1922.
Le Poesie (1913 - 1947) — Frammenti lirici, Poesie sparse, Canti anonimi, Poesie religiose—raccolte ed edite a cura di Piero Rebora. Vallecchi, Firenze, 1947.
Le Poesie (1913 - 1957) —Frammenti lirici, Canti anonimi, Canti dell'infermità, Poesie varie—a cura di Vanni Scheiwiller. All'Insegna del Pesce d'oro, Milano, 1961.
Lettere (1893 - 1930), a cura di Margherita Marchione. Prefazione di Carlo Bo. Edizioni di Storia e Letteratura, Roma, 1976.
L. Andreyev. *Lazzaro e altre novelle.* Vallecchi, Firenze, 1919.
L. Tolstoi. *La felicità domestica.* La Voce, Firenze, 1920; II ediz. Bompiani, Milano, 1942; III ediz. Mursia, Milano, 1960; IV ediz. Bompiani, 1965.
N. Gogol. *Il cappotto.* Il Convegno Editoriale, Milano, 1922.
Colui che ci esaudisce (Gianardana). Caddeo, Milano, 1923. (Collezione universale, n. 91 - 92, versione, cenno, note e commento di Clemente Rebora). Edizione di lusso con illustrazioni e fregi di Alberto Salietti, Bottega di Poesia, Milano s.d. [1922].

SECONDARY SOURCES

BETOCCHI, CARLO. "Su Clemente Rebora," *Il Frontespizio,* Firenze, IX, no. 4, 1937. An important, critical examination of Rebora's early poetry.
———. "Considerazioni di oggi sulla poesia di Clemente Rebora," *L'Approdo,* Torino, 1952. A reevaluation of the importance of Rebora's poetry.
Bo, CARLO. "Disegno d'una poesia," *Maestrale,* Roma, I, no. 2, 1940. Reprinted in *Nuovi studi.* Firenze: Vallecchi, 1942. The first of several fundamental articles. See *Lettere di Clemente Rebora,* 1977, Preface by Carlo Bo, pp. v - xiii.

Selected Bibliography

BOINE, GIOVANNI. "Plausi e botte," *Riviera Ligure,* Oneglia, XX, no. 33, 1914. Reprinted in *Il Peccato e le altre Opere,* edited by Giancarlo Vigorelli, Parma: Guanda, 1971. This is the most important and fundamental analysis of Rebora's poetry.

CECCHI, EMILIO. "Esercizi ed aspirazioni," *La Tribuna,* Roma, 1913. A review of *Frammenti lirici* which classifies Rebora as an Idealist.

CHADOURNE, LOUIS. "Clemente Rebora: *Frammenti lirici,*" *France-Italie,* Paris/Firenze, I, no. 5, 1913. Written in French, this article stresses the Idealism found in Rebora's poetry.

CONTINI, GIANFRANCO. "Due poeti d'anteguerra: Dino Campana, Clemente Rebora," *Letteratura,* I, No. 4, 1937. Reprinted in *Esercizi di lettura.* Firenze: Parenti, 1939. Contini was the first critic to emphasize the qualities and characteristics of Rebora's language.

COSTANZO, MARIO. "Clemente Rebora," *Itinerari,* II, no. 9 - 10, Genova, 1954. Reprinted in *Studi critici.* Roma: Bardi, 1955. Rebora's cultural formation is discussed.

DEFEO, ITALO. "Il mondo di Rebora," *Radiocorriere,* 1977. The recently published *Lettere di Clemente Rebora* is reviewed and readers are reminded of the indelible mark left by Rebora on Italian poetry.

DEL SERRA, MAURA. *Clemente Rebora: lo specchio e il fuoco,* Vita e Pensiero, 1976. A reexamination of Rebora's religious poetry.

FABIANI, ENZO. "Questa Suora è un ciclone," *Gente,* Milano, 1977. This is an interview with the editor of *Lettere di Clemente Rebora.*

FRATTINI, ALBERTO. "Dante in Rebora," *L'Osservatore Romano,* Roma, 1977. References to Dante are found in Rebora's poetry as well as in *Per un Leopardi mal noto.*

GETTO, GIOVANNI. "L'ultimo Rebora," *Ausonia,* Siena, XI, No. 21, 1956. Reprinted in *Stagione,* Roma, 1957. Analysis of the religious poetry Rebora wrote after his conversion.

GOLINO, CARLO. *Contemporary Italian Poetry, An Anthology,* Foreword by Salvatore Quasimodo, University of California Press, 1962. Contains two of Rebora's poems: "Campana di Lombardia" (Lombardy Bell) and "Dall'Imagine tesa" (With Tense Imagination) by Carlo Golino, pp. 38 - 41.

GUGLIELMINETTI, MARZIANO. *Clemente Rebora.* Milano: Mursia, 1961. A perceptive excursus of Rebora's life, divided into three periods.

LOLLO, RENATA. *La scelta tremenda. Santità e poesia nell'itinerario spirituale di Clemente Rebora.* Milano: I.P.L., 1967. A study of the relationship between Rebora's religious vocation and his poetry.

MARCHIONE, MARGHERITA. "Clemente Rebora prosatore," *La Fiera Letteraria,* Roma, 14:12, 1959. A study of Rebora's prose with emphasis on his correspondence and the originality of its language.

———. "La storia d'amore di Clemente Rebora," *La Fiera Letteraria,*

14:39, Roma, 1959. The article includes nine unpublished poems dedicated to Lydia Natus, a Russian pianist.

———. "Scritti di guerra," *Ecclesia,* 18:9, Rome, 1959. The various periodicals where Rebora's poetic prose writings appeared in the years 1916 - 1918.

———. "Linguaggio reboriano," *Lingua nostra,* 20:3, Firenze, 1959. A study of Rebora's dynamic language.

———. *L'imagine tesa, La vita e l'opera di Clemente Rebora,* Prefazione di Giuseppe Prezzolini. Roma: Edizioni di Storia e Letteratura, 1960. Reprinted and updated in 1974. Clemente Rebora the literary figure is portrayed against the background of his spiritual itinerary, with attention to the many interrelations that bind his lyrics to his prose and letters.

———. "Carteggio inedito di Clemente Rebora e Giuseppe Prezzolini," *Stagione,* Roma, 1961. A lengthy introduction about the friendship between Rebora and Prezzolini is followed by twenty-two unpublished letters (1909 - 1923).

———. "Clemente Rebora," *Italian Quarterly,* XII, 46, California, 1968. The life and works of Rebora are treated in English, with some unpublished material and photographs of the poet.

———. "Four Poems," *Forum Italicum,* Buffalo, 1969. The English translation of four poems by Rebora: "Corale notturno" (Choral Nocturne), "L'ultimo trillo" (The Last Trill), "Dall'Imagine tesa" (From the tense image), "Terribile ritornare a questo mondo," (It is difficult to come back to this world).

———. "Clemente Rebora nel panorama letterario," *Rassegna di politica e di storia,* Roma, 1969. An examination of the position of Rebora in 20th century poetry and a brief summary of his life and works.

———. "L'altro amore di Clemente Rebora," *La Nuova Antologia,* Roma, 1970. On the friendship between Sibilla Aleramo and Clemente Rebora, followed by sixteen unpublished letters.

———. "Clemente Rebora," *Forum,* Indiana, 1971. A critical analysis of Rebora's poetry with a brief resumé of his life.

———. "Rebora e Meriano," *Quaderni dell'Airone,* Capua, 1973. A lengthy article with unpublished letters by Rebora to Francesco Meriano.

———. "Rebora e Furlotti," *L'Osservatore politico-letterario,* Milano, April 1974. A study of the friendship between Rebora and Bruno Furlotti.

———. *Twentieth Century Italian Poetry,* edited and translated by Margherita Marchione with illustrations by Filomena Puglisi. Rutherford, N.J.: Fairleigh Dickinson Press, 1974. Of the ninety poems, sixteen are by Clemente Rebora.

MARTINI, CARLO. "Clemente Rebora traduttore dal russo," *Persona,*

Roma. In 1971, the January-February issue of *Persona* was dedicated to Clemente Rebora and contained articles by Francesco Grisi, Gianluca Prosperi, Fausto Montanari, Lavinia Mazzucchetti, Artal Mazzotti, Claudia Lazzerotti Ottaviani, Carmelina Sicari, Clemente Riva, Angelo Barile, Carlo Martini.

MONTEVERDI, ANGELO. "Clemente Rebora: *Frammenti lirici,*" *La Voce,* Firenze, VI, No. 7. 1914. An analysis of Rebora's early poetry.

PALIERI ANNESI, GIULIANA. "L'Epistolario di Clemente Rebora," *Osservatore della Domenica,* Roma, 1977. A reevaluation of his life and poetry, twenty years after his death.

PETRUCCI, ANTONIO. "Lettere di Rebora," *L'Osservatore Romano,* Roma, 1977. A discussion of the importance of Rebora's correspondence.

PREZZOLINI, GIUSEPPE. "Rebora e la suora americana," *La Nazione,* Firenze, 1957. Reprinted in *Il Tempo,* Roma and *Il Resto del Carlino,* Bologna. A revealing article on Prezzolini's last visit with Rebora.

———. *Il tempo della Voce.* Milano/Firenze: Longanesi/Vallecchi, 1960. Rebora is included among the important writers of the twentieth century who contributed to *La Voce.*

———. "I doveri dei parenti degli uomini illustri," *La Fiera Letteraria,* Roma, 1961. A series of articles defending the book, *L'Imagine tesa,* and Rebora's friendship with Lydia Natus.

———. "Omaggio a Rebora," *Il Resto del Carlino,* 1976, Bologna. The first of many reviews of the book, *Lettere di Clemente Rebora.*

REBORA, PIERO. "Clemente Rebora e la sua prima formazione esistenzialista," *Humanitas,* Brescia, February 1959. An important article which discusses the existential qualities of Rebora's poetry.

SALA, VINCENZO. "La prima santità di Rebora," *L'Azione,* Novara, 1977. An analysis of Rebora's letters written before his conversion revealing his early search for Truth.

Index

"*A Silvia,*" 59 - 60
Abbo, John A., 160n9
Accademia Libera di Cultura ed Arte, 116
Accademia Scientifico-Letteraria, 25, 26, 36, 42, 49, 146
Aleramo, Sibilla, 80, 85, 90, 91, 163n5
Alfieri, Vittorio, 31, 160n4
Allegria dei naufragi, (Ungaretti), 22
Almanacco della Voce, (ed. Prezzolini), 47
Ambrosini, Luigi, 46
Amendola, Giovanni, 46, 47, 162n5
Ammaestramenti morali di Fra Jacopone, (ed. Piero Rebora), 168n10
Anceschi, Luciano, 17
Andreyev, Leonid, 81, 82, 83, 163n8
Angelini, Cesare, 16, 17, 113, 153n2, 161n1
"*Anima Errante,*" 131
Anthologie des poètes italiens contemporains, (Chuzeville), 172n12
Apollinaire, Guillaume, 83
Apollonio, Mario, 148
"*Arche di Noè sul sangue,*" 95
Armonie della vita umana, (ed. Linacher)
Avanti!, 145

Balkan Wars, The, 88
Banfi, Antonio, 15, 25, 27, 37, 41, 42, 43, 52, 71, 77, 138, 158n7
Baudelaire, Charles, 21
Beatrice, 141, 142
Beethoven, 78
Begey, Maria Bersano, 168n10
Beilinson, 168n10
Belloni, G.A., 32

Belti, Remo Bessero, 148
Bene nella natura umana, Il (Solovjòv), 168n10
Betocchi, Carlo, 17, 147
Biblioteca Brera (Milan), 41
Binazzi, Bino, 141, 164n10
"*Bizzarria e corale di retrovia,*" 95
Böhme, Jacob, 168n10
Boine, Giovanni, 21, 22, 46, 49, 79, 89, 143, 146, 147, 155n19
Borgese, G.A., 154n4
Brigata, La, 83, 89, 94, 95, 140, 141
Bruers, A., 168n10
Bruno, Giordano, 31, 49, 146, 150, 159n2
Bucci, Vincenzo, 145
Buddha, 31
Buzzi, Paolo, 20, 154n11

"*Calendario,*" 95
"*Campana di Lombardi,*" 101 - 102, 147
Campana, Dino, 21, 22, 155n17
Campanella, Tommaso, 49, 146, 150
Camperio, Meyer (Signora), 113 - 114
Camposampiero, Carlo, 147
Canti dell'infermità, 125 - 129, 147
Cantideva, 168n10
"*Canto di donna*", 61 - 62
"*Canzoncina*", 97, 98 - 99
Caporetto, 88
Cappotto, Il (The Overcoat), (Gogol), 84 - 85
Capristo, Giovanni, 169n17
Carbonari, 108, 167n1
Carducci, Giosuè, 19, 20, 63, 153n1
Carducciani, 19, 20, 21, 62
Carnevali, Emanuel, 147
Carrà, Carlo, 16

178

Index

Carteggio Giovanni Boine, (ed. Margherita Marchione - S.E. Scalia) 155n19
Cary, Joseph, 154n12
Cascella, Michele, 16, 91
Case of the Casa Italiana, The (Prezzolini), 154n14
Casnati, Francesco, 17
Cecchi, Emilio, 17, 33, 46, 145
Chadourne, Louis, 33, 145
"Chiesola dello Spielberg, La", 133
Chiminelli, Piero, 168n10
Christ, 31, 78
Chuzeville, Jean, 172n12
Circolo del Convegno, 113
Circolo Filologico Femminile, 116
"Cittadella" Award, 130, 136
Civiltà Cattolica, 172n17
Classicism, 19
"Clemente, non fare cosi!", 25, 70 - 73, 100, 141
Clemente Rebora (Guglielminetti), 148
Clemente Rebora: lo specchio e il fuoco (Maura del Serra), 148
Coari, Adelaide, 121, 141, 146, 168n11
Collegio Borromeo, 17
Collegio Rosmini, 15
Columbia University, 15
"Consolatore, Il", 66 - 67
Conti, Primo, 135
Contini, Gianfranco, 147
"Corale notturno", 65
Corazzini, Sergio, 19
"Coro a bocca chiusa", 95
Corriere della Sera, 145
Cossacks, The (Tolstoi), 83 - 84
Costanzo, Mario, 17, 134
Crepuscolarism, 19, 20
Croce, Benedetto, 46, 147
Cultura dell'anima (ed., Papini), 49
Curriculum Vitae, 28, 120 - 121, 123, 130 - 132

"Dall'imagine tesa", 105 - 107, 119, 147
Dannunziani, 19, 20, 21
D'Annunzio, Gabriele, 19, 20, 60, 90, 154n3
Dante, 49, 57, 134, 142, 146, 150
De Robertis, Giuseppe, 145, 147

Diana, La, 89
Diario Sentimentale della Guerra (Sentimental Diary of the War) (Panzini), 48, 89
"Dio ci lasciò vedere l'Italia", 94
Discorsi Militari (Boine), 89
Dolce Stil Novo, 23, 150
Dominicis, Armando, 153n4
Dostoevski, Feodor, 81, 83, 164n15
"Duties of Man, The" (Mazzini), 111

Enrica (niece), 75, 95
"Equal vita diversa urge intorno, L' ", 51 - 53

Fabiani, Enzo, 16
Falqui, Enrico, 16, 147
"Fantasia di carnevale", 70
Fascism, 168n13
Fede dell'avvenire, La (Guyau), 168n10
Felicità domestica, La (Family Happiness) (Tolstoi), 83
Fogazzaro, Antonio, 167n2
"Fonte nella macerie", 95
Frammenti lirici, 33, 47, 49, 50, 51 - 69, 110
France-Italie, 33, 145
Frontespizio, 147
Furlotti, Bruno, 139, 140
Futurism 20 - 21, 145, 171n8

Galbusera, Carlo, 25
Gallarati Scotti, Tommaso, 16, 44, 113, 167n2
Galletti Alfredo, 16, 147
Gargiulo, Alfredo, 147
Garibaldi, Giuseppe, 24, 108, 142, 158n3
Gentile, Giovanni, 46, 169n15
"Gesù il Fedele", 142
Gioberti, V., 168n10
"Giorni dispersi", 57 - 58
Giovane Italia, La, 158n1, 167n1
Gobetti, Piero, 82
Gogol, Nikolai, 81, 84, 85, 164n19
Golino, Carlo, 23
Gorlago, 90
Govoni, Corrado, 20, 101, 154n10
Gozzano, Guido, 19
"Gran grido, Il", 142

Gruppo d'Azione, 111
Guglielminetti, Marziano, 148
Guinizelli, Guido, 145
Guyau, G.M., 168n10

Hermet, Augusto, 168n10
Hermetic Poetry, 156n21
Heroici furori, (Giordano Bruno) 159n2

Idealism, 56, 160n9
Imagine Tesa, L' (Marchione), 148, 153n1
In cammino verso la luce (Cantideva), 168n10
"*In orario perfetto*", 95
Ina (niece), 95
Inferno (Dante), 92
"*Infinito*" (Leopardi), 52
"*Invisibile Amore, L'* ", 69
"*Italia*" (Gogol), 85, 164 - 165n20
Italia, la Chiesa e la Civiltà universale, L' (Gioberti), 168n10

Jacopone da Todi, 23, 157n29
Jahier, Piero, 21, 22, 46, 49, 89, 155n20
Janârdana (Colui che ci esaudisce - Gianardana), 115, 116, 121
Jansenism, 34

Lambruschini, R., 168n10
Lattes, D., 168n10
Lazzaro e altre novelle (Lazarus and Other Stories) (Andreyev), 82
Leonardo, 51
Leopardi Giacomo, 23, 31, 49, 52, 59, 60, 61, 146, 150, 157n26
Les Noces (Villageoises) (Stravinsky), 83
Lettere (1893 - 1930) (ed. Margherita Marchione) 148, 153n5
Lettere familiari (ed. Piero Rebora), 148
Letters to a Young Poet (Rilke), 140
Lettura, La, 89
Libreria della Voce, 46
Libretti di Vita, 116 - 117
Linacher, A., 168n10
Lo Gatto, Ettore, 164n20, 168n10

Lollo, Renata, 148
Loveno, 30, 91
"*Lucciola, io ti chiudevo*", 86

Malaguzzi, Daria, 26, 27, 35, 42, 43, 44, 91, 148, 158n6
Mameli, 169n16
Manìa dell'Eterno (letters and unpublished documents), 148
Manualetto di rettorica (Panzini), 47
Manzoni, Alessandro, 169n9
Marchione, Margherita, 15 - 18, 113, 148
Marinetti, Filippo Tommaso, 20, 154n9, 171n8
Martini, Carlo, 172n9
Martorano, Giuseppe (captain), 93, 94
"Mater Clementissima", 133
Matteotti, Giacomo, 117, 169n15
Mazzini, Giuseppe, 24, 33, 100, 108, 112, 113, 115, 116, 118, 142, 158n1, 167n1, 169n16
Mazzinianism, 56, 116, 139
Mazzucchetti, Lavinia, 25, 33, 92, 159n7
Meriano, Francesco, 82, 83, 94, 139, 140, 164n10
"*Mia voce, La*", 67 - 68
Michaelstädter, Carlo, 21
Michelangelo, 49, 146
Mignon, Maurice, 172n12
Mill, John Stuart, 143, 171n14
Mombello Hospital, 139
Momigliano, Attilio, 147
Momigliano, Eucardio, 145
Montale, Eugenio, 17, 22, 156n24
Monteverdi, Angelo. 15, 25, 27, 28, 29, 33, 36, 37, 38, 39, 42, 46, 77, 94, 144, 158n7
Montini, Giovanni Battista (Pope Paul VI), 125
Moretti, Marino, 19, 70
Mount Podgora, 89, 91, 92, 96, 140
"*Movimenti di poesia*", 75 - 77, 86, 133
Murri, Romolo, 46
Mussolini, 168n13

National Association for the Mezzogiorno (The South), 44, 109

Index

Natus, Lydia, 27, 75 - 78, 79 - 81, 84, 85 - 87, 93, 98 - 99, 163n1
Negri, Ada, 163n1
"Nella seral turchina oscurità", 53 - 56
Nietzsche, Friedrich, 20, 48, 49, 78
Nobel Prize, 156n24, 157n25
"Non ardito perchè ardente", 100 - 101
"Notte a bandoliera", 70
"Notturno", 127 - 128
Novati, Francesco, 37, 160n4

"O carro vuoto sul binario morto", 28, 62 - 63
Overcoat, The (Il Cappotto) (Gogol), 84, 85
Onofri, Arturo, 21, 22, 155n18

"Paglia, La", 25, 27
Palazzeschi, Aldo, 19, 49, 101
Palmieri, A., 168n10
Pancrazi, Pietro, 172n11
Panzini, Alfredo, 47, 48, 89, 91
Papini, Giovanni, 17, 22, 46, 49, 155n15, 162n2
Parnassians, 20
Parodi, G.B., 146
Pascal, Blaise, 106, 166n1
Pascoli, Giovanni, 19, 20, 60, 101, 153n2
Pascoliani, 19, 20, 21
Péguy, Charles, 146
Pellico, Silvio, 133
"Pensateci ancora", 95
"Per l'acre fluir dei minuti", 32, 56 - 57
"Perdono?", 94, 95
"Pesce, come fuor d'acqua boccheggi!", 143
Petrarca Francesco, 23, 157n27
Plotino, 168n10
Poe, Edgar Allan, 101
Poesie, Le, 134 - 136
"Poesia e santità", 136, 142
Poeti d'oggi (Papini-Pancrazi), 172n11
Political Thought: Men and Ideas (Abbo), 160n9
Popolo, Il, 16
Pound, Ezra, 137, 170n13
"Pozzo e la lucciola, Il", 86

"Preludio ai Canti dell'infermità", 126
Prezzolini, Giuseppe, 15, 16, 34, 42, 44, 46 - 47, 48, 49, 70, 73, 83, 90, 119, 143, 145, 147, 154n14, 161n1
"Prima del sonno", 134
Primo Rebora, Il (ed. by Daria Banfi Malaguzzi), 148
Promessi Sposi, I., 169n9
"Più belle pagine dei poeti d'oggi, Le", 147

Quasimodo, Salvatore, 22, 157n25

Raccolta, La, 89
Radiocorriere, 50
Rebora, Clemente (1885 - 1957), and Boine, 21, 22, 46, 49, 79, 89, 143, 146, 147, 155n19; and Mazzini, 108 - 12; and Prezzolini, 15 - 17; 46 - 47; conversion, 119 - 24; correspondence, 17 - 18, 119 - 24; critics, 145 - 149; dissertation on Romagnosi, 32 - 34; early life and studies, 24 - 27; literary revolution, 23; love for music, 27 - 28; Lydia Natus, 27, 75 - 78, 79 - 81, 84, 85 - 87, 93, 98 - 99, 163n3; military service, 28; missionary spirit, 44; mountain-climbing, 29; political attitude, 117 - 18; relationship with father, 30 - 32; self-portrait, 28 - 29; teacher, 35 - 40; war experiences, 88 - 89

WORKS - POETRY:
 Canti anonimi, 100 - 107
 Canti dell'infermità, 125 - 129
 Curriculum vitae, 17, 28, 47, 120, 123, 130, 137
 Frammenti lirici, 33, 47, 49, 50, 51 - 69, 70, 110, 145
 Poesie varie, 70 - 78

WORK - PROSE:
 Bontà, ragazzi e Voce (risposta a nessuna domanda), "Goodness, Boys and *La Voce* (answer to no question)", 48
 Libretti di vita (ed), 116

Rettorica di un umorista, La (The Rhetoric of a Humorist), 47
Scritti di guerra, 94 - 95
Semplici nozioni di grammatica italiana ("Simple Elements of Italian grammar"), 47
Vita che va a scuola e vice versa, La "Life that goes to school and vice versa"), 48

WORKS - TRANSLATIONS:
Cappotto, Il, 84 - 85
Felicita domestica, La, 83 - 84
Janàrdâna, Colui che ci esaudisce (Gianardana), 114 - 16
Lazzaro e altre novelle, 82 - 83
Rebora, Enrico (father), 30 - 32
Rebora, Teresa, (mother), 24, 71, 92
Rebora, Marcellina (sister), 72, 76
Rebora, Piero (brother), 16, 33, 50, 71, 77, 117, 121, 122, 132, 133, 134, 135, 143, 147, 148, 168n10
Reggio Calabria, 44, 109
Regola di Santo Benedetto (ed. Hermet), 168n10
Regole e il testamento di San Francesco, Le (ed. Hermet), 168n10
Rilke, Rainer Maria, 140
Rimbaud, Arthur, 136, 170n12
Rinnovamento, Il, 162n4
Risorgimento, 34, 108, 142
"*Ritmo della campagna in città, Il*", 70, 73 - 75
Riviera Ligure, 49, 147
Rivista d'Italia, 33, 60
Rivoluzione liberale, La, 82
Romagnosi, Giandomenico, 30 - 34, 35, 49, 119, 159n1
Romanticism, 19
Roncalli, Angelo Giuseppe (Pope John XXIII), 121
Rosmini, Antonio, 33, 119, 130, 138, 158n2
Rosmini Fathers, 15, 24, 122, 123, 124, 132, 133, 134, 135
Rossi, Cesarina, 42
Rossi, Vittorio, 147
Rusconi, Bice, 139, 141

Saba, Umberto, 49

"*Sacchi a terra*", 102 - 104
Sàdhanà, 114
Saggezza cinese (ed. Tucci), 168n10
Saggio, Carlo, 16
Saint Clare, 141, 142
Saint Francis, 142
Salvemini, Gaetano, 46
Sbarbaro, Camillo, 46, 49
"*Scampanìo con gli angioli*", 95
Scelta tremenda, La (Lollo), 148
Scheiwiller, Gianni, 136, 137
Scherillo, Michele, 37, 160n5
Schuster, Ildefonso (Cardinal), 121, 123, 169n7
Scienza nuova (Vico) 159n3
Scillitan Martyrs, 120, 169n4
"*Sconfitta*", 58
Scritti di Guerra, 94 - 99
Scritti di religione (ed. Banfi), 168n10
Scritti per la conferenza mondiale delle chiese cristiane (ed. Palmieri), 168n10
Scritti religiosi dei riformatori italiani del 1500 (Chiminelli), 168n10
Scuola Martignoni, 116
"*Sempre più in là*", 64
Semprini, Giovanni, 168n10
Senza Approdo (Cesarina Rossi), 42
"*Sera estiva*", 62
"*Serenata del rospo*", 97 - 98
Serra, Renato, 46
Siotto-Pintor, General, 90
Slataper, Scipio, 46
Soffici, Ardengo, 22, 46, 155n16
"*Soffrire*", 32, 58 - 61
Solovjòv, V., 168n10
Spagnoletti, Giacinto, 17, 21, 147
"*Speranza*", 127
Spirito e l'azione, Lo (Maria Bersano Begey), 168n10
"*Stralcio*", 95
Stravinsky, Igor, 83

Tagore, Rabindranath, 114, 168n4
Tales of a Hurried Man (Carnevali), 147
Tempo, Il, 16
"*Tempo*", 96 - 97
Tempra, La, 89

Index

"*Terribile ritornare a questo mondo,*" 125
"*Territoriale consigliato, Il*", 94 - 95
Tiepolo, Giovanni Battista, 113
Titta Rosa, G., 17
Tolstoi, Leo, 81, 83, 84, 164n12
Towianski, 116, 168n10
Treviglio, 37, 38, 40
Tribuna, La, 33
Tucci, G., 168n10
Turco-Italian War, 73, 88

"*Ultimo trillo, L'* ", 66
Umanità (Banfi), 169n15
Ungaretti, Giuseppe, 22, 156n22
University of Santiniketan (Bengal, India), 114

Valeri, Diego, 131, 148
Vallecchi, Enrico, 147
Verità ti libererà (ed. Semprini), 168n10
"*Viatico*", 96
Vico, Giovanni Battista, 31, 159n3
Voce, La, 21 - 22, 32, 44, 46 - 50, 56, 89 - 90, 130, 138, 146, 150
Volpe, Gioacchino, 16, 32, 146, 172n9
von Hügel, Friedrich, 155n19, 167n2

Zanotti Bianco, Umberto, 44
Zapelloni, Carlo, 148
Zibaldone (Leopardi), 139
Zuccante, Mariuccia, 27

THE LIBRARY
ST. MARY'S COLLEGE OF MARYLAND
ST. MARY'S CITY, MARYLAND 20686